The Resilient Voter

Voting, Elections, and the Political Process

Series Editors: Shauna Reilly and Stacy G. Ulbig

Receptive to studies in the American and comparative settings, the *Voting, Elections, and the Political Process* series examines the broadly defined electoral process. The series seeks scholarly monographs and edited volumes that investigate the ways in which voters, candidates, elected officials, parties, interest groups, the media, and others interact in the context of electoral politics. Works with a focus on individual attitudes and behavior, institutional and contextual influences, and the legal aspects of the electoral process are welcome. This series accepts interdisciplinary work using a variety of methodological approaches.

Recent Titles

The Resilient Voter

Stressful Polling Places and Voting Behavior

Shauna Reilly and Stacy G. Ulbig

LEXINGTON BOOKS
Lanham • Boulder • New York • London

Published by Lexington Books
An imprint of The Rowman & Littlefield Publishing Group, Inc.
4501 Forbes Boulevard, Suite 200, Lanham, Maryland 20706
www.rowman.com

Unit A, Whitacre Mews, 26-34 Stannary Street, London SE11 4AB

British Library Cataloguing in Publication Information Available

Library of Congress Cataloging-in-Publication Data

Names: Reilly, Shauna, 1980– author. | Ulbig, Stacy G., author.
Title: The resilient voter : stressful polling places and voting behavior / Shauna Reilly and Stacy Ulbig.
Description: Lanham : Lexington Books, [2018] | Series: Voting, elections, and the political process | Includes bibliographical references and index.
Identifiers: LCCN 2017059041 (print) | LCCN 2017055790 (ebook) | ISBN 9781498533539 (electronic) | ISBN 9781498533522 (cloth : alk. paper)
Subjects: LCSH: Voting—United States. | Polling places—United States. | Elections—United States. | Political participation—United States. | Political psychology—United States.
Classification: LCC JK1967 (print) | LCC JK1967 .R35 2018 (ebook) | DDC 324.6/5—dc23
LC record available at https://lccn.loc.gov/2017059041

∞ ™ The paper used in this publication meets the minimum requirements of American National Standard for Information Sciences—Permanence of Paper for Printed Library Materials, ANSI/NISO Z39.48-1992.

Printed in the United States of America

Contents

List of Figures

List of Tables

Acknowledgments

Our first project together, this book was a testament to working collaboratively and problem solving without a history upon which to build. Without question, this was a positive working relationship and a true partnership. While only our names are on the cover of this book, many others assisted us with this project, and we are grateful for their assistance.

First, we are grateful to our colleagues. We would especially like to thank Richard N. Engstrom, who introduced us to each other and started this collaboration, as well as being instrumental in research design, coding decisions, data collection, and variable coding. His insight and contributions, as well as ongoing moral support, throughout our work on this project provided a solid foundation on which we further developed this project. His calm demeanor and sense of humor buoyed our spirits at key moments. Throughout this endeavor, he was, as always, among the most relaxed individuals on earth—second only to Jeffrey "The Dude" Lebowski in our estimation.

We also thank Jeffrey Zimmerman and Thomas "Phil" Milewski who assisted with the initial proposal and the preliminary experiment at NKU, as well as Tammy Lee and Surin Ann for their assistance with the final experiment. The Midwest, Southern, American, and Southwest Political Science Associations provided all-important externally imposed deadlines and discussants who provided valuable feedback on individual chapters that both kept us on task and ensured us to keep an eye on the quality and thoroughness of the product.

Shauna would also like to thank Dr. Shamima Ahmed, former Chair of Political Science, Criminal Justice and Organizational Leadership for her support and encouragement. Her leadership and advice has guided Shauna's career and propelled future scholarship. I am forever in her debt. Additionally, Tonya Krouse for her biweekly check-ins to ensure timely completion.

In similar fashion, Stacy would like to express her gratitude to Shauna and Rich for inviting her into this project, as well as her everlasting thanks to Rhonda Callaway, Heather Evans, Tom Haase, Faith Demiroz, and Ken McIntyre for their encouragement and counsel throughout the duration of this project.

Finally, financial assistance allowed us to complete the experiment. We would like to thank the Northern Kentucky Undergraduate Research Council for funding the preliminary experiment that helped refine the questions and process. Likewise, the Department of Political Science and College of Humanities and Social Science at Sam Houston State University financially supported the study described in this book, as well as Dr. Ulbig's associated travel. Similarly, we must acknowledge Northern Kentucky University's College of Arts and Sciences' professional development fund and the Department of Political Science, Criminal Justice and Organizational Leadership for providing financial assistance in support of travel to professional conferences and for helping Dr. Reilly make it to the great state of Texas to conduct the experiment.

Chapter 1

Voting Barriers

The Obstacle Course of
Electoral Participation

"It was just chaos," reported the *Los Angeles Times* (June 7, 2016). "Long lines, registration issues complicate voting," screamed a *Washington Post* headline (November 9, 2016). "Provisional ballots denied to voters," declared the *Washington Post* (November 9, 2016). In Nebraska, the *Omaha World-Herald* warned voters, "Read it carefully: Ballot language for death penalty referendum is correct, but confusing" (September 20, 2016). The 2016 election season certainly offered the media, political candidates, and the public a surfeit of opportunities to pontificate about the potential damage inflicted on American democracy by the use of complicated ballot language, the implementation of provisional ballot laws, and long lines at polling places. While the election that pitted a real-estate mogul and television personality against the first female nominee of a major political party for president was certainly unique in many ways, the polling place tumult highlighted by so many was not a contemporary anomaly.

Elections of the past decade have produced an increasing number of reports about voters frustrated and demobilized by long lines (Dao, Fessenden, and Zeller 2004) and registration problems experienced by as many as one in eight potential voters (Powell and Slevin 2004). In the media coverage of the 2016 elections, reporters detailed long lines, computer glitches and voter intimidation (see Foreman, Spink, and Habersham 2016, for example). Elections are run on a state and county level, which decentralizes the responsibility for making adjustments to precincts and ballots. Voting reforms have also opened the door to make the voting process more onerous. The responsibility for knowing more details about the election process and how to overcome polling place barriers frequently falls to the voters. The traditional voting booth has changed—processes are more electronic, different rules guide the absentee ballot process, voters can vote prior to Election Day in some states

1

and even vote by mail. All of these activities change the way that voting has been conducted, yet the impact of these has not been fully discussed in the literature.

Cost and efficiency continue to permeate the election process. County officials, particularly in rural counties, simply do not have the resources or experience to handle computing and other requirements for electronic ballots, late voter registration, provisional ballots, and so forth. The temporary precinct workers often have little training or experience for electronic environments and for handling the complicated rules now in place. Voters, in some constituencies, are squeezed into fewer polling places, increasing some of the problems we investigate in this book. These activities designed to save resources and in some cases required to facilitate Election Day have consequences. In this book we seek to examine the ways in which the anxiety potentially produced by such polling place stressors might affect the decisions voters make when casting their ballots. Could the polling place problems lamented in recent elections represent an important external force that adversely affects voters at the very moment they should most focus on casting complete ballots supportive of their political preferences? We investigate the possibility that complicated ballot language, provisional voting, and long polling place lines cause some voters to cast ballots in a manner contradictory to their preferences. That is, we ask whether polling place conditions might cause voters to become so frustrated and anxious that they inadvertently cast a vote that does not support their desired electoral outcome.

We argue that such polling place barriers place citizens under stress that can prevent them from casting a complete ballot or choosing to vote at all. Further, we contend that even when they are able to endure these stressors to cast a ballot, the anxiety produced might adversely affect their ability to vote in a manner consistent with their standing policy preferences. We test these assertions by experimentally investigating the ways in which long lines, registration difficulties, and complex ballot language affect voters' willingness to complete the whole ballot and their ability to cast ballots consistent with their preferences. To our surprise, we find that voters prove remarkably resilient in the face of the sorts of potentially stressful polling place barriers highlighted in recent elections. Our unexpected findings, however, are not all good news for the democratic process in America. Though many voters are able to weather the conditions at stressful polling places, certain segments of the voting public appear to be more vulnerable to their negative influences.

A PRICE TOO HIGH? STRESSFUL BARRIERS TO VOTING

Many worry that increasing levels of polling place pandemonium and confusion will drive potential voters away from the voting booth, and this certainly does seem plausible. Individually or combined, factors such as those listed above can work to create a stressful polling place atmosphere that some may choose to avoid altogether. As evidenced by recent high levels of voter turnout, however, many endure the polling place mayhem in order to cast their ballots. Electoral impediments, though, might still present problems by placing stress on voters at the very moment they need to be motivated and focused on casting ballots.

The notion that bedlam at the polls might prevent some from voting is not an especially novel idea. More than half a century ago, Anthony Downs explained declining voter turnout in terms of a negative cost-benefit calculation on the part of the electorate. A potential voter viewing the act of voting as conferring more benefits than costs will likely cast a ballot, but someone seeing more costs than benefits to voting will likely bypass the polls. While the potential benefits accompanying voting—a candidate of choice winning, favorable policies being enacted, etc.—were readily imaginable to many at the time, the costs of voting were often seen as minimal, perhaps nonexistent. As a result, many were stumped as to why turnout in US elections was not higher. Downs pointed out that the costs of voting can actually be quite high, especially once one considers the chance of a single vote deciding the entire election.

Studies of voting behavior over the intervening years have highlighted the impact that a number of potential barriers to voting might have on turnout. Of the institutional factors scrutinized by political scientists, perhaps no other has received as much attention as voter registration requirements. For almost a century, scholars have argued that difficult registration procedures keep voters away from the polls (see, e.g., Merriam and Gosnell 1924; Wolfinger and Rosenstone 1980). For most nascent voters, registration represents the earliest, and often insurmountable, barrier encountered. And the United States is one of the few countries where the burden to register falls completely on voters themselves (Powell 1986). Voters in some states must register themselves with the secretary of state or board of elections 30 days in advance of Election Day. Additionally, some states add a burden for participation in the primary where voters must indicate their partisan preferences by the end of calendar year ahead of the primary election (see Kentucky laws as an example). Adding a residency requirement to advance registration raises the hurdle to be cleared before voting even higher (Berinsky 2005; Brians and Grofman 1999; Franklin 1999; McDonald and Samples 2006), especially for those who relocate close to Election Day. Like many voting barriers, registration requirements tend to disproportionally affect the minority, poor, and less-educated segments of the potential electorate (Rosenstone and Hansen 1993). While some studies report that eased registration requirements can increase turnout (Brians and Grofman 1999) and yield a more demographically representative electorate (Piven and Cloward 1988), not all programs aimed at lowering the registration barrier seem to work equally well. Neither Election Day registration nor "motor voter" registration methods considered beneficial to the populations historically most disadvantaged by registration requirements, have increased turnout as posited (Knack 1995; Neiheisel and Burden 2012).

External factors more proximate to Election Day, particularly campaign-related activities, have been shown to more closely relate to voter behavior. For instance, campaign intensity, most likely due an increased information about candidates, has been shown to improve voters' ability to vote consistently with their political preferences (Bergbower 2014; Lau and Redlawsk 1997). Similarly, researchers have repeatedly established a link between negative campaign advertising and both voter turnout and vote choice (e.g., Doherty 2014; Stevens et al. 2008). And a well-established line of investigation into the voter mobilization activities of parties (e.g., Huckfeldt and Sprague 1992; Kramer 1970; Krassa 1988, 1989) and community activists (Gerber and Green 2008) has established the influence these groups can have on voters.

Even Election Day conditions unrelated to the campaigns themselves can play some role. For instance, a number of studies suggest that adverse weather conditions on Election Day can drive down turnout (Gatrell and Bierly 2002; Gomez, Hansford, and Krause 2007; Shachar and Nalebuff 1999). There are perhaps no external factors more proximate to the moment of vote choice than conditions at the actual polling place, and in fact, frustrations encountered at the polling place have been shown to drive away voters. Distant and difficult-to-access polling places, as well as those that are moved (Brady and McNulty 2011; Gibson et al. 2013; Gimpel and Schuknecht 2003; McNulty et al 2009), "lower-quality" precincts (Barreto, Cohen-Marks, and Woods 2009; Haspel and Knotts 2005), and long lines at the polling place (Highton 2006), appear to deter voter participation. At the same time, creating a festive atmosphere around the polling place (Addonizio, Green, and Glaser 2007) or using more conveniently located polling centers (Stein and Vonnahme 2008) seems to entice voters to go to the polls. There is even some evidence that polling place context can affect decision-making, with voters exposed to religious imagery expressing less support for abortion-related issues (Rutchick 2010).

VOTING "CORRECTLY"

While these studies have demonstrated the effects that even small obstacles to voting can have on voter turnout, few address the issue of vote choice beyond asking questions about whether higher turnout would redound to the benefit of one party or candidate. After all, the secret nature of the Australian ballot used in US elections impedes the ability of researchers to observe the actual vote choices made by individual voters. We believe, however, that the potential polling place barriers that have plagued recent elections might be affecting not only those who failed to cast a ballot but also those who fought their way through the complicated ballot language, provisional ballots, and long lines that stood in their path on the way to casting a ballot.

The ability of citizens to cast ballots in a manner consistent with their policy preferences is paramount to democracy. We expect that more direct public voting on public-policy decisions stands on the foundation of the underlying preferences of voters. Thus, citizens must have some preferences in terms of these policy decisions and should be able to distinguish their preference among the policy options with which they are confronted.

Those who focus on the ability of the voting public to cast ballots in ways that accurately reflect their preferences have coined the term *voting correctly*.[1] This should not be taken as a statement on the quality or content of a vote in a normative sense, but rather, it focuses on whether voters actually cast ballots that accurately reflect their voting preference for either candidates (Lau and Redlawsk 1997) or ballot measures (Lupia 1994a, 1994b, 2001).

Accurate voting appears to be more common on candidates than on ballot measures (e.g., policy referenda, proposed amendments). Research illustrates that voters use a variety of cues (Lupia 1994a, 1994b, 2001; Bowler and Donovan 1998; Lau and Redlawsk 1997) to cast ballots consistent with their policy preferences. In addition to being less salient to voters, ballot proposition elections carry the additional burden of making specific laws, which can prove daunting to voters. Still, when it comes to making informed choices, research indicates that voters are generally able to make decisions consistent with their policy preferences both on candidates (Lau and Redlawsk 1997) and on ballot questions (Lupia 1994a, 1994b, 2001; Bowler and Donovan 1998). We wish to add to this literature by examining the ways in which different obstacles encountered at the polling place may limit voters' ability to cast ballots in a manner supportive of their policy preferences.

The idea that voters participate in ballot measures and races and do not vote consistently with their policy preference has been often studied. Lau and Redlawsk (1997) found that even under the condition of perfect information, citizens voted incorrectly about 25 percent of the time in presidential elections between 1972 and 1988. They determined vote "correctness" by comparing the voters' values, beliefs, and knowledge to their candidate choices, as revealed on a survey of 293 respondents. Based on survey responses, they determined that races with fewer candidates showed a higher level of voting consistency. Senatorial races have been shown to have even higher instances of inconsistent voting than presidential elections, most likely due to lower candidate saliency and more limited information availability (Bergbower 2014).

Further work within the subfield of correct voting shows that additional information and exposure to information about the political issues at play in an election can help citizens vote more consistently with their preferences. Whether it is political interactions on social media or the distribution of formal news through social media outlets, increases in political knowledge appear to provide voters with heuristic cues that serve as mental shortcuts to arriving at the "correct" vote (Sokhey and McClurg 2012; Ryan 2011). Races with high levels of campaign spending have been associated with incorrect voting (Richey 2013). Similarly, campaign intensity acts as a buffer against incorrect voting (Bergbower 2014), and even casual political conversation and political discussion (Richey 2008) can help guide voters in casting votes that support their underlying beliefs and preferences.

One of the more often studied aspects of consistent voting in elections is voting on policy proposals instead of candidates. Some find that voters are able to vote in a manner consistent with their policy preferences (Bowler and Donovan 1998; Lupia 1994), perhaps through the use of certain simple voting cues (Lau and Redlawsk 1997). It seems that, despite limited information, citizens made thoughtful responses to referenda questions, even using limited cues (Lupia 1994a, 1994b). Despite the belief that citizens are ignorant, they did have some knowledge about government and were able to make reasonable ("correct" or "sincere") decisions about complex questions. Still, there are a number of factors that can complicate the use of such cues and contribute to inconsistencies in voting.

Other studies remind us of the important caveat that the actual language used on the ballot can present a complication for voters facing policy proposals. Reilly (2010) and Reilly and Richey (2011) found that complex ballot language affects participants' ability to cast a ballot and to vote consistently with their preferences. Voters also show a tendency to vote against a ballot measure just because it is complexly worded. And, given the low saliency of most ballot measures, what is on the ballot often represents the only information a voter receives (Harmon 2010). Unfortunately, the text of ballot measures may not always fairly and accurately summarize the underlying policy proposals behind the measure (Burnett and Kogan 2015), or it may be too complex for voters to understand clearly (Reilly 2010; Reilly and Richey 2011), especially when combined with framing effects of endorsements

(Burnett and Kogan 2015). The butterfly ballot used in Florida in 2000, for example, was notorious for confusing voters and possibly leading them to vote erroneously (Dillman 2002; Lausen 2008), but other design issues can prove important as well. Instruction wording and placement, for instance, has been shown to influence voters (Laskowski and Redish 2006), as has paper ballot design (Everett, Byrne, and Greene 2006; Reynolds and Steenbergen 2006). While researchers have given electronic voting mechanisms a lot of attention (Alvarez, Ansolabehere, and Stewart 2005; Kropf and Kimball 2013), ballot type and design seem to be more closely associated with errors in voting (Knack and Kimball 2003; Kimball and Kropf 2005; Herrnson, Hanmer, and Niemi 2012). Incidents such as the butterfly ballot in Florida, as well as interstate inconsistencies in ballot design (Niemi and Herrnson 2003), bring into question the ability of all Americans to meaningfully participate in the democratic process (Niemi and Hernson 2003).

OUR STUDY

Taken together, these results highlight not only the error-proneness of American voters, especially when making more complex decisions with limited information, but also the role that external influences, including complex ballot language, can play in voter decision-making. And it is on these findings that we wished to build. While the researchers we discussed here do not explicitly acknowledge the role of anxiety in voter decision-making, they do indicate that the electorate is susceptible to external forces that can alter their vote choices. We build on this work by investigating the possibility that polling place problems of complicated ballot language, the use of provisional ballots, and long waits at the polling might cause voters to cast incomplete ballots and/or cast votes in a manner inconsistent with their previously stated policy preferences.

We sought to better understand the role that external stressors encountered at the polling place play in voter decision-making on policy referenda ballot questions of different complexity. While studies of this nature generally rely on self-reports of vote choice either before or after the voter casts his or her ballot, we believe that such examinations miss an important part of the story—mistakes made in the ballot booth. Voters who inadvertently cast votes that are inconsistent with their previously stated preference can hardly be expected to report that they did so when asked. Consequently, we designed our study so that we could directly examine the ballots of each participant and compare his or her vote choices to preferences revealed on a survey prior to Election Day.

We extend previous studies by examining not only the ways in which ballot language might affect the ability of voters to *vote correctly* but also the ways in which the use of provisional ballots and long waits at the polling place might add to the confusion that complicated ballot language can cause in the voting booth. While some have argued that both of these potential polling place factors put voters under conditions that cause them to abstain from voting altogether, we investigated the possibility that provisional ballot use and polling place wait times may also affect those voters who withstand the inconveniences and frustrations they cause to cast a ballot.

We further chose to focus on voting in direct democracy elections rather than candidate elections. Voting on ballot measures such as proposed constitutional amendments offers a more complex voting situation than choosing from among a small number of candidates. Voters may choose a particular candidate for a variety of reasons, including partisan loyalty or the personal appeal of a particular candidate, which tends to serve as a strong voting cue that is likely to withstand many complicating factors. Less salient ballot proposal elections offer fewer voting cues on which voters can rely on when it comes to voting on policy matters as compared to candidates. Consequently, we focused on voting for proposed state constitutional amendments, which offer voters fewer voting cues and are more likely to be directly connected to the policy preferences of voters rather than a personal connection to a party or candidate. For example, a voter who states a pro-life stance should be expected to vote against proposed amendments that extend abortion rights and in support of proposals that add restrictions to abortion. In contrast, a voter who holds an affection for his or her incumbent officeholder (or his or her party) is likely to cast a ballot in support of the candidate even if their policy preferences diverge.

PLAN OF THE BOOK

In the next chapter, we set out the theoretical underpinnings of the book, suggesting that polling place barriers put citizens under stress that can not only prevent them from voting but also influence their ability to vote in a manner consistent with their policy preferences. The third chapter provides details about our experimental research design as well as our measurement strategies for key variables in our analyses that follow. In the fourth chapter, we report findings from an experiment designed to test the effects of ballot language complexity through examination of the impact that ballot measure readability and topic have on the ability of voters to cast ballots supportive of their previously stated policy preferences. We illustrate the ways in which ballot language complexity can stress voters and affect their behavior in the voting booth. We further investigate the ways in which such effects might cause particular trouble for certain kinds of voters. Building on our findings about ballot language complexity, chapter 5 provides an introduction to voter identification laws and electoral practices that have increased the use of provisional ballots. We examine the impact that the use of such ballots might have on voters by investigating the question of whether provisional ballot use distracts and upsets voters, resulting in incomplete balloting and inconsistencies between voting preferences and vote choice. Next, we evaluate the effect that polling place waiting can have on voting quality in chapter 6. We test assertions about longer wait time leading to the casting of incomplete ballots or ballots that do not support previously stated policy preferences. In our last investigatory chapter, we explore the ways in which certain voter and election official characteristics might interact with ballot language complexity, provisional ballot use, and polling place wait times to better understand the ways in which these barriers might place a heavier burden on certain segments of the electorate. We conclude by summarizing our results from the previous chapters, addressing potential shortcomings of our research design, and discussing some possible implications of our research.

Before beginning our investigation of the ways in which polling place conditions might affect the ability of voters to cast correct votes, we first turn to the question of why such things might affect voters at the moment they mark their ballots. It is to this task that we turn in the next chapter by reviewing the stresses associated with decision-making as well as the evidence of stress at work in the electorate and stating our expectations with regard to ballot language, provisional voting, and long waits at the polling place.

NOTE

1. We chose to reframe this by calling votes consistent with policy preferences "conformity" to avoid the perception that we are making normative judgments about the "right" way to vote on the ballot issues.

Chapter 2

Sweating the Vote

Polling Place Stress as a Voting Barrier

The effects that voting barriers exert on voter turnout have typically been explained in a Downsian framework where voters weigh the relative costs and benefits of voting. Since any additional cost to voting can rather easily exceed the small probability of a single vote deciding the election, the inconveniences of registering, becoming informed about the issues and candidates involved in the election, and, finally, locating and getting to the polling place, lead to a decline in turnout. Similarly, the material and social benefits of such things as festival activities help offset the costs of voting, increasing the number who make it to the polls. We do not argue with this logic. We believe that ballot complexity, provisional ballot use, and long polling place wait times represent additional costs to voting that might affect the public's willingness to cast votes and the ability of voters to cast ballots that accurately reflect their preferences. We first address the question of why voters might see these polling place hassles as highly costly.

THE STRESSES OF DECISION-MAKING

The answer may lie in the psychology of stress. Psychological research demonstrates that stress is an environmental condition (Janis and Mann 1977; Keinan 1987) with which decision makers must contend in most decision-making scenarios (Kowalski-Trakofler, Vaught and Scharf 2003). Further, researchers suggest that individuals respond to stressful situations by attempting to avoid them (e.g., Janis and Mann 1977). When avoidance is not possible, individuals attempt to cope with stressors by employing a vigilant pattern of sound and rational decision-making targeted at relieving the stress (Janis and Mann 1977). In the Downsian framework, individuals seek to minimize the costs of stress. Studies provide some evidence that when faced with controllable stressors, that is, those that can be removed or attenuated with good decision-making, individuals are able to respond with vigilant, and better, decision-making (see, e.g., Janis 1982; Keinan 1987).

Less controllable stressors, however, can impair individual decision-making capabilities (Janis 1982; Janis, Defares, and Grossman 1982; Keinan 1987). That is, unavoidable stressors can tax cognitive processing skills, adding costs to the task of voting. Under such pressure, decision makers tend to narrow their attention, excluding potentially important information (Bacon 1974; Baddeley 1972; Hockey 1970; Kahneman 1973; Weltman, Smith, and Egstrom 1971). Consequently, stressed individuals might reach a faulty decision because not all the relevant alternatives are considered (Janis 1982; Sieber 1974; Wright 1974; Wright and Weitz 1977). Further, the information brought under consideration in such situations is often processed in a disorganized manner (Janis 1982; Keinan 1987; Wachtel 1967). Combined, these tendencies lead to poor decision-making outcomes.

While much of the psychological research focuses on immediate physical stressors, these stress-coping tendencies can readily be extrapolated to the political realm where less concrete stressors often play a prominent role. Research into elite decision-making has investigated the influences of such intangible pressures. Scholars in the field of international relations have long studied the ways in which leaders respond to stress when making foreign policy decisions. Building on the psychological findings, these researchers argue that stress can negatively impact decision-making (e.g., Hermann 1979; George 1980). In this context, stress appears to cause "impaired attention and perception" that leads heads of state to take a "shortened and narrow perspective" when making stress-laden foreign policy decisions (George 1980, 49; see also Holsti 1984, 68). In the American setting, research on presidential decision-making has included stress studies (e.g., George 1980; Sigelman and McNeil 1980).

STRESS IN THE ELECTORATE

We argue that in the same ways stress can adversely affect elite decision-making, it can also affect the public. While there has been limited research on stress as it affects individual voters, there is a robust line of research investigating the electorate's response to national tragedies, suggesting this is the case. Following the devastation of the 9/11 terrorist attacks in New York City, there was a measurable increase in public concern for national security (Kaiser and Moore 2001). In this same period, President Bush's approval rating reached its apex. Similarly, in New Orleans elections following Hurricane

Katrina, citizens who experienced a more significant amount of flooding were also more likely to vote in the following mayoral election (Sinclair, Hall and Alvarez 2011). In a more extreme example, some research alludes to the ability of stress disorders following traumatic events (i.e., posttraumatic stress disorder) to alter voting patterns (Ben-Erza et al 2013). Thus, stress appears to exert some pressure on voters' cognitive processing of information during election season.

Building on this research, we argue that a stressful context at the polling place can affect voters' ability to cast a ballot consistent with their policy preferences. When faced with a stressful Election Day environment, potential voters might attempt to avoid the situation. Having already arrived at the polling place, voters might simply choose to walk away or, alternatively, engage in roll-off behavior, that is, begin casting a ballot and then quit before making decisions in all races. At the same time, stressed voters attempting to cast a ballot are likely to succumb to the psychological pressures of the situation, and consequently make poorer voting decisions. It is the latter two possibilities that we examine here.

Stress on the voter can come from a variety of sources, including a lengthy wait at the polling place, and voter registration problems. Additional time spent standing in line at the polling place puts voters under pressure to complete other time-sensitive tasks and thus adds costs to the act of voting. Similarly, registration problems encountered at the polling place can be frustrating and anger provoking. Beyond the costs and stresses of registering well ahead of the election, there are additional causes of voter stress, such as locating a potential voter's name on the voter roll, being required to provide the correct identification, and facing challenges to one's right to vote in the election. These place additional burdens on voters that are likely to result in feelings of stress. Finally, not all voting decisions are created equal. Some votes are simply easier to cast than others, with complicated ballots demanding more cognitive processing than simpler ones. A confusing ballot layout or complicated ballot language will likely add to both the stress of the voting act and the demands made of the voters, affecting their decision-making (see, e.g., Reilly 2010; Reilly and Richey 2011).

Voters who reanalyze the calculus of voting under any, and certainly all of these, circumstances will likely become more apathetic about casting a ballot and perhaps choose to abandon the task of voting in favor of pursuits believed to be more beneficial. Even those who choose to persevere and cast a ballot are likely to experience increased voting costs and impaired decisional capabilities. While the benefits of voting for particular candidates in high-profile elections might still outweigh these additional stress-induced costs, spending even more time in an unpleasant situation in order to vote in races further down the ballot—especially those that are confusing—is less likely. Thus, voters who have become emotionally and/or mentally drained even before they enter the voting booth might be more likely to cast an incomplete ballot.

For those voters who do not abandon the ballot partway through, we might expect to see poorer decision-making under stressful conditions. After all, stressed voters are likely to narrow the volume of information they consider and to process the information they consider in a disorganized, and ultimately less helpful, manner. Thus, our most general hypothesis asserts that when confronted with obstacles during the task of voting, those experiencing stress at the polling place will be more likely to cast incomplete ballots and to vote inconsistently with their previously stated preferences.

HYPOTHESES

When subjected to barriers at the voting booth (such as long lines and challenges about their right to vote), voters become emotionally/mentally drained even before they enter the voting booth and are consequently driven to cast votes only in more prominent races, such as presidential or gubernatorial contests. The causes and consequences of voter stress are paramount to understanding the effects of events on Election Day. Voters who encounter obstacles will report more stress on Election Day than those who do not. Often, these obstacles are created by administrators—inability to find names on the registration list, inability to direct voters to the correct precinct, or even taking too long to process voters, thus lengthening the time it takes to vote.

Hypothesis 1: Subjects who encounter an obstacle caused by an administrator (provisional ballot/long wait) will report more stress.

Researchers have shown that simply going to a polling place is stressful (Waismel-Manor, Ifergane, and Cohen 2011) and that voting in a public place (versus at home via absentee ballot) elicits more of the stress-related hormone cortisol (Niemen et al. 2015). The added burden of having one's voting rights publicly challenged and being denied the right to cast a traditional ballot likely drives up the baseline level of stress associated with voting. And as the research reviewed earlier suggests, those experiencing higher levels of stress can find their cognitive capacities impaired. Thus, we sought to test for the effects that provisional ballots may have on producing additional stress and diminished decision-making skills among those asked to complete them. We first expected participants who were questioned about their registration status, asked for additional identification, and asked to complete a provisional ballot to report feelings about their electoral experience that were more negative.

As the psychological literature informs us, individuals respond to stressful situations in a variety of ways. When possible, they simply avoid them (e.g., Janis and Mann 1977). Thus, we might expect provisional voters to be less likely to complete their ballots than other voters. Those who do choose to complete the ballot may want to move through the process quickly to avoid further anxiety. Reading and completing a ballot more quickly can result in lowered comprehension and mistakes in marking the ballot. Further, heightened stress has been shown to impair cognitive reasoning by limiting the amount of information brought to bear on a decision, excluding potentially important information, and processing the information that is used in a disorganized manner (see chapter 1 for details). Combined, these tendencies lead to poor decision-making outcomes. Thus, we hypothesized that mock voters asked to complete a provisional ballot would be more likely to cast incomplete ballots and less likely to vote consistently with their previously expressed preferences.

Participants who face long waits may be demoralized by the process and only vote for the top race, rather than working their way through the ballot to some of the less prominent races. Additionally, as voters have already waited for a lengthy period of time, they may not want to spend time in the polling location voting throughout the ballot as well as reading and understanding complex measures. Further, those who do take the time to read the ballot face obstacles in the form of ballot language.

Hypothesis 2: Subjects who encounter barriers at the poll location will be more likely to exhibit roll-off behavior.

A confusing ballot layout or complicated ballot language will likely both add to the stress of the voting act and place additional demands on voters, ultimately affecting their decision-making (see, e.g., Reilly 2010; Reilly and Richey 2011). When confronted with complicated passages that describe various legal and policy issues, voters may come to doubt the efficacy of their vote and worry about their naiveté regarding the issue. Consequently, they may choose to abstain from casting a vote. Complicated ballot language also serves to obfuscate the issue and confuse voters. A voter may not be familiar with the legalese—or other terminology—provided on the ballot, making the language, and thus ballot, inaccessible. This further complicates the voting task and can lead to mistakes when voting.

Similarly, the barriers presented by provisional ballots and polling place wait times, likely to be exacerbated by encounters with election administrators, were also expected to cause delays and frustration at the polling place that further stress voters, leading to fatigue and/or a tendency to rush in casting a ballot, both of which can lead to the casting of incomplete ballots.

Just as top-of-ballot races such as those for president or governor have more salience and garner more media attention in the lead-up to the election, we expected ballot measures presented closer to the top of the ballot to be more salient to our mock voters. Consequently, we believed that those facing polling place barriers, whether based on ballot language or on experiences upon arrival at the polling place, would be less likely to fight their way through the ballot and accordingly be less likely to participate in ballot proposals presented down ballot.

Hypothesis 3: Subjects who encounter barriers at the poll location will be more likely to vote inconsistently.

While ballot language continues to be a challenge for voters, we also added two variables to determine what increased effect they may have on roll-off and conformity. We expected that those participants who were exposed to the variables of long waiting lines or provisional ballots would have higher levels of roll-off and less conformity between policy preferences and votes than those who were not exposed to these conditions. These additional barriers at the voting booth would affect voters, as they would already be frazzled by the treatment and less likely to read carefully and vote consistently with their policy preferences. Additionally, because of the extra time associated with these obstacles, they would be less likely to vote on all of the measures presented on the ballot.

Alternatively, they might be more committed to voting at that point, as they had already overcome obstacles to voting. The literature suggests that those who do overcome barriers are more committed to the voting process and more likely to participate in elections down the road (Hajnal, Gerber, and Louch 2002). For those voters who did not abandon the ballot partway through, we could expect to see poorer decision-making under the conditions of the barriers before them. Consistent with established findings, we expected such voters to be more likely to cast ballots against their previously stated preferences (i.e., to vote incorrectly), due to their inclination to narrow the volume of information they considered and the disorganized, and ultimately less helpful, manner in which they processed it.

Since nonsalient topics have been shown to affect voter participation, the topic of the direct democracy election can be an important factor. As some researchers have noted, there are times when voters are particularly familiar with a ballot proposition topic due to its saliency, campaign information, or deeply held opinions (Nicholson 2003, 2005; Lupia 1994a, 1994b, 2001). Thus, when facing what is known as an "easy" issue (Carmines and Stimson 1980), voters will be able to overcome the barrier created by ballot language complexity. Easy issues are those understood by the public at an emotional or "gut" level (and are opposed to "hard" issues that require greater political interest and understanding). Because voters will be more familiar with an easy issue, they can use their instincts to overcome the problems presented by the complexity of the ballot language.[1] Therefore, we hypothesized that the effects of ballot language complexity were likely to differ between easy and hard issues.

Hypothesis 4: Voters will be more likely to vote consistently on ballot measures stated in less complex language.

Election administrators often shoulder the blame for the problems voters encounter at the polls. Although frequently undertrained, poll workers represent the street-level administrators, and likely the *only* election officials, the public interacts with on Election Day. Consequently, interactions with these poll workers can have a lasting impact on voters' mental states as they cast their ballots, possibly affecting their willingness to complete the ballot and their ability to vote in a way that supports their previously expressed preferences. We evaluate this hypothesis in chapters 5 and 6. Further, we argue that participants who were asked to wait or given a provisional ballot would report more negative feelings toward the administrators because they received such treatment. Essentially, the treatment provided to participants (albeit randomly) may reflect on the administrator in a negative way.

Not all voters are alike, however. Research tells us that race, education level, and income can greatly affect one's ability to make voting decisions—both whether to vote and how to vote (Rosenstone and Hansen 1993; Campbell et al. 1960). This is particularly true when looking at minority voters and direct democracy. The context of these types of elections tends to be more harmful to minority voters and they may be directly or indirectly targeted by this legislation (Tolbert and Hero 1996; Donovan and Bowler 1998; Hajnal, Gerber and Louch 2002; Branton 2004). When racially relevant or charged ballot measures are presented to voters, minorities tend to vote as a bloc, and in ways expected to protect themselves (Branton 2004; Bowler, Nicholson and Segura 2006). However, when that environment is not racially charged or there is race-neutrality on the measure then there is no consistent impact on minority voters (Branton 2004).

Further, we suggest that the administrator who provided the ballot or presented the barrier would impact the ability of subjects to vote consistently. The stress on voters caused by the process may be exacerbated by who they interact with. If the administrator is someone they can relate to, they may be able to overcome the barrier more easily than if it is someone who they are uncomfortable with or who is different from them.

Hypothesis 5: The effects of polling place barriers are likely to vary for voters of different races and ages, administrator characteristics, voter experience, and feelings about the important of voting.

The literature demonstrates that there are certain populations that are more likely to use provisional ballots, especially transient and minority voters (Alvarez and Hall 2009). Furthermore, precincts with younger residents show a higher rate of provisional balloting (Alvarez and Hall 2009). Thus, we expected certain socioeconomic factors to influence the effect that provisional ballots have on voters. In fact, our experimental participants represented a racially diverse, young (college-aged) group, precisely the demographics we might expect to change households frequently (Bleemer et al. 2014). Thus, we expected race and age to show a stronger relationship to both roll-off and voting conformity among the group that voted provisionally.

In particular, minority voters are less likely to participate and more likely to roll off down ballot (Barreto and Ramirez 2004; Branton 2003, 2004; Citrin and Green 1990; Gamble 1997; Hero 1998; Hero and Tolbert 1996; Magleby 1984; Vanderleuw and Engstrom 1987). Although there are lower voting rates for minorities during candidate races, minorities' participation rates on ballot measures are even lower than in local-level elections (Vanderleeuw and Sowers 2007). An explanation may lie in the types of ballot measures proposed. There is a history of racially motivated ballot measures and those aimed at limiting the rights of minorities (e.g., Arlington 1990; Lewis 2011; Haider-Markel, Querze, and Lindaman 2007; Gunn 1981; Tolbert and Hero 1996).[2] As a result, voters may have a valid reason to participate in some but not all ballot measures.

However, there is a paradox in minority participation on ballot propositions. While they may not participate on ballot measures at the same rates as their white counterparts, when minorities do participate, they exhibit high levels of conformity. Hajnal, Gerber, and Louch (2002) examined minority votes on ballot propositions. They found that minority voters in California tend to vote as cohesive blocks on ballot propositions and are often on the winning side of the vote. There are several possible reasons for this cohesion. First, campaigns often target specific groups, providing them with low-cost information about ballot measures. Minority voters targeted in this manner may use cues from elites to help formulate their policy preferences and vote on specific issues. While Hajnal, Gerber, and Louch's (2002) research was limited to California, they found that minority voters are more likely to vote on measures that they care about, and when they do vote, they exhibit high levels of group unity. This is particularly true on racially relevant ballot measures (Branton 2004). Thus, we expected that although there might be higher levels of roll-off for these voters, when they do participate, their votes would closely align with their policy preferences. Similarly, younger voters have different priorities and experiences with voting. Younger voters are more likely to move frequently and are more susceptible to provisional ballot provisions.

Further, voters who have more commitment to the process are often more likely to be frequent voters and participate often. Frequent voters have been exposed to election issues, such as those in this study, and are more able to overcome polling place complications, as they are more familiar with the voting process. Thus we expected, participants who see voting as more important would be better able to overcome the effects of ballot complexity (chapter 4), provisional ballot use (chapter 5), and longer polling place wait times (chapter 6). We investigate these hypotheses in chapter 7.

Ballot measures have been found to limit the participation of minority groups (Vanderleeuw and Engstrom 1987), which could be particularly true when these groups are exposed to a various levels of complexity in ballot language on a single ballot (Reilly and Richey 2011; Reilly 2010). Previous studies have shown that education and race are important considerations in who participates in direct democracy elections (Branton 2003; Vanderleeuw and Engstrom 1987). Branton's study includes three election periods, where she finds support for racial and socioeconomic causation that has been previously discussed in voting literature (Campbell et al. 1960) and reiterated for race in the direct democracy literature (Vanderleeuw and Engstrom 1987). The findings that socioeconomic status and race play a role in participation in direct democracy are unsurprising, as voters who participate in other elections will have an expected higher rate of participation in direct democracy elections. This effect is expected in direct democracy elections, perhaps even more so than in representative elections, because of the higher levels of engagement and political knowledge that are required to vote on these measures. Therefore, these measures often limit the power of the people, whose opinions are being sought in these elections, demonstrating the importance of this experiment in the larger picture of participation and voting on ballot measures for all groups.

Hypothesis 5.1: Subject socioeconomic status affects the scope of the barrier.

Minority voters prefer fewer races on ballots and typically shy away from ballot propositions. Thus, we see lower levels of voting in direct democracy elections as a whole from minority voters (Barreto and Ramirez 2004; Branton 2003; Vanderleeuw and Engstrom 1987; Magleby 1984). This effect is more evident for ballot measure elections than it is for lower-level elections on the ballot (Vanderleeuw and Sowers 2007). Further, while minority voters may be more likely to roll off the ballot, they are less likely to vote against their interests on ballot measures when they do vote (Hajnal, Gerber, and Louch 2002). Thus, we hypothesized that while there may be higher levels of roll-off for non-white voters, when they do participate, minority mock voters will cast ballots that closely align with their policy preferences. As demonstrated in the literature, some groups are more at risk to roll off when it comes to ballot questions. One could presume that there may be connections between specific groups and the ability to conform votes with policy preferences in a similar fashion. For example, there may be race and ethnicity effects as well as language barriers that can influence voter participation.

Hypothesis 5.1a: Minority voters facing polling place obstacles will exhibit higher levels of ballot roll-off and lower voting consistency.

Research on youth voters creates an interesting subset in the literature. The literature on youth voting indicates that the easier it is for young people to vote, the more likely they are to participate (Fitzgerald 2003). This refers to registration barriers and convenience voting; as such, we would expect that youth voters who face obstacles at the polls would be more likely to roll off. Though limited, research on youth voting in direct democracy shows that young voters tend to be more interested in ballot questions that have high saliency and are connected to widespread campaigns (Donovan, Tolbert, and Smith 2009). Youth tend to take cues from their socialization process on voting in elections (Gentry 2010; Pacheco 2008). Thus, ballot measures are a more burdensome type of election for youth voters, particularly in a vacuum, and could result in less participation in these types of elections. Youth voters also tend to be very critical and distrusting of the electoral process (Dermody, Hammer-Lloyd, and Scullion 2010). Such attitudes and behavior likely translate to policy votes, such as a ballot measure where the language is more complex and challenging to understand. As a result, we would expect that youth voters would be less likely to support ballot measures as a whole.

Hypothesis 5.1b: Younger voters facing polling place obstacles will exhibit higher levels of ballot roll-off and lower voting consistency.

The election administrator has a large impact on the use of provisional ballots and, thus, the ability to vote consistently. As the literature demonstrates (Alvarez and Hall 2006; Cobb and Hedges 2004; Kimball and Foley 2009), many of the decisions about the use of provisional ballots are left up to undertrained poll workers. And their interactions with voters often lower the voters' efficacy and trust in the voting process (Hall, Monson, and Patterson 2009). So the frontline worker administering the election at the polling place can have a dramatic impact on the use of provisional ballots. To investigate a number of potential administrator effects, we took advantage of our experimental design and the variation of both our subjects and our mock election administrators. We employed five different mock election administrators with varied demographic characteristics, including diversity in age, sex, race/ethnicity, and regional residency. This variation coupled with the diversity of our subjects allowed us to investigate potential effects that the race and sex of the election administrator might exert as well as the ways in which demographic similarity between mock voter and administrator might affect the impact of provisional ballots. These are explored in hypothesis 5.2 and its sub-hypotheses.

Hypothesis 5.2: Administrator traits affect voter stress levels and consistency.

Hypothesis 5.2a: Voters facing polling place obstacles and encountering a minority election administrator will exhibit higher levels of stress and lower voting consistency.

We also examined the effect of racial homogeneity. Building on the argument that people, in general, prefer interactions with similar others, Costa and Kahn (2003, 3) argue "members of minority groups may prefer to interact with other minority members if they fear discrimination." Others suggest that minorities often face the choice of interacting with and joining heterogeneous groups (in terms of civic engagement) where they will always be a minority or not participating at all (Alesina and La Ferrara 2000). In the context of America's long history of racial discrimination at the polling place and heightened media attention to such claims in recent elections, we investigated whether voters would be more comfortable with an administrator who shares their racial/ethnic identity. Thus, we expected mock provisional voters who encountered an administrator of a different race/ethnicity to report higher levels of stress, and consequently more ballot roll-off and lower voting consistency, than those who faced an administrator of the same race/ethnicity.

Hypothesis 5.2b: Voters facing polling place obstacles and encountering an election administrator of the same race will exhibit lower levels of stress and higher voting consistency.

The literature also suggests that there is a consistent effect of women who administer polling interviews: women tend to get more negative reports from respondents (Groves and Fultz 1985). Further, subjects tend to express support for more egalitarian issues and female issues when the interviewer is female (Kane and Macaulay 1993; Leuptow, Moser, and Pendleton 1990).

While our participants did not respond to the administrator directly, we expected the same negativity found with Groves and Fultz (1985) as well as the inconsistency or modification of their vote (as seen in interview research in Kane and Macaulay 1993; Leuptow, Moser, and Pendleton 1990) when the administrator was female. We expected mock provisional voters who encountered a female administrator to report higher levels of stress, and consequently more ballot roll-off and lower voting consistency, than those who faced a male administrator.

Hypothesis 5.2c: Voters facing polling place obstacles and encountering a female election administrator will exhibit higher levels of stress and lower voting consistency.

Turning to the ways in which cultural congruity between voter and administrator might condition the impact of provisional ballots, we investigated the ways in which shared race and regional identification between voter and administrator might mitigate the stress associated with provisional ballots. As others have pointed out, people prefer to interact with others similar to themselves (Costa and Kahn 2003). Since our experiment was conducted in the South and the participants either hailed from the South or had been living in the South while attending classes, we expected most of our mock voters to more readily identify with our two Southern administrators than with the three non-Southerners. Even those who are not native or long-time denizens of Dixie often claim the demeanor of Southerners and Southern culture (Key 1949) can seem less confrontational than those of other regions. Taken together, these conditions may have made our mock provisional voters more comfortable with the process and less reactionary to the questioning of their voting rights when challenged by a Southern mock election official. Thus, we expected mock provisional voters who encountered a Southern administrator to report lower levels of stress, and consequently less ballot roll-off and higher voting consistency, than those who faced a non-Southern administrator.

Hypothesis 5.2d: Voters facing polling place obstacles and encountering a Southern election administrator will exhibit lower levels of stress and higher voting consistency.

At the same time, not all participants in the experiment would view voting in the same manner. We hypothesized that those who placed a higher level of importance on voting would be able to overcome the ballot complexity because they would work harder to understand and mediate the effects of the ballot language. Those who did not see voting as important would make less thoughtful responses and would not deliberate over the consequences of their vote as much because they did not value the process in the same way.

Hypothesis 6: Subject experience and valuation of voting influences the effect of the barrier.

Familiarity often makes the process easier for voters. Frequent voters, familiar with the electoral process, have experienced various activities on Election Day and are more likely to understand both the requirements (e.g., photo identification, prior registration) and potential complications that voting entails. Thus, we hypothesized that voters who had more experience in voting would be less affected by ballot complexity. Voters who had been exposed to ballot propositions and other electoral situations might be more likely to overcome the barriers in the voting booth, specifically complex language, because they had experience with these types of elections. By being familiar with ballot propositions, voters might understand terminology and be less susceptible to the stress of voting. Further, those who participate in elections more frequently are also likely to have clearer ideological and issue preferences Experienced voters and those who feel voting is important may be more readily equipped to overcome obstacles they encounter at the polling place.

Hypothesis 6.1: Voters who have voted more frequently in the past will exhibit higher voting consistency than those who have voted less frequently in the past, even when facing polling place barriers.

Similarly, those who feel voting is important, even if they do not have a long history of voting in previous elections, are likely to have paid particular attention to relevant voting requirements. Thus, we expected subjects who encountered obstacles and reported frequently voting in the past and those who felt voting was more important to report lower stress levels, and consequently higher voting consistency, than those who reported not voting as frequently in the past or who felt that voting was not as important.

Hypothesis 6.2: Voters who feel voting is more important will exhibit higher voting consistency than those who feel voting is less important, even when facing polling place barriers.

We report our findings regarding these hypotheses in the remainder of this book. First, however, we explain our approach to studying questions about polling place barriers. In the next chapter, we first provide a general introduction to basic research strategies and justify our use of an experimental approach while also acknowledging the limitations such an approach brings with it. We next explain the way in which we conducted our study, providing a description of the sample of subjects we studied, explaining several of our measurement strategies with regard to key variables that are used in chapters 4–6, and providing an introduction to the analytical techniques we will employ in those chapters.

NOTES

1. One could argue that a campaign would add to saliency, as there may be coverage about certain measures that provide additional material to overcome the complexity of the ballot language. However, since we are testing these hypotheses in an experiment external factors such as a campaign are moot.

2. Other research, however, suggests that minorities are not necessarily hurt by ballot measures and the vast majority of these measures actually do not specifically impact minority voters (Haider-Markel, Querze, and Lindaman 2007; Hajnal, Gerber, and Louch 2002).

Chapter 3

Studying Polling Place Stress

An Experimental Approach

There are numerous approaches to the study of political behavior, particularly voting. A long line of research in the field asks questions about overall voter engagement using aggregate-level turnout statistics to compare mass voter participation across jurisdictions and/or over time. Others examine individual-level voting behavior with data collected from a variety of sources, including myriad types of public opinion surveys, publicly available official registration and voting records, and even biological measures. Some scholars study voters in actual elections, while others study mock voters in simulated election environments. Each approach has its own set of advantages and disadvantages, with no one offering an ideal investigatory approach for all questions. The "best" research strategy depends on, among other things, the question asked. A researcher learns little about the effect of individual-level partisanship on the decision to vote by examining turnout statistics for the nation as a whole, for instance. Consequently, political scientists must be careful to match their methodological approach to their inquiry.

In a very general sense, researchers take an experimental, nonexperimental, or quasi-experimental approach toward the study of their questions. Experimental researchers simulate an electoral experience and study the behavior of their subjects. Subjects in Ansolabehere and Iyengar's (1995) investigation of the effects of negative political advertising, for instance, watched short television news segments with imbedded political ads that differed in tone in a laboratory setting. In contrast, those taking a nonexperimental approach observe the behavior of voters in actual elections or "in the field." Asking questions similar to those of Ansolabehere and Iyengar, Kahn and Kenny (2004) investigated negativity in the US Senate Campaigns using survey data from a nationally representative sample of voters. While an experimental design allows for control of extraneous influences better than a nonexperimental one, it also takes place in an artificial environment and often relies on subjects who might not be fully representative of the general electorate. Conversely, a nonexperimental field study offers a look at real voters in real elections but offers little control of countless factors that might affect voters' behavior.

The limitations of each approach have led some researchers to combine the two. Those researchers using a hybrid, quasi-experimental method study real voters while also imposing some experimental elements or control. Researchers will often take advantage of a naturally occurring event to conduct a field experiment as Mondak (1995) did when he studied the voters' knowledge in the context of a newspaper strike that affected Pittsburgh but not Cleveland. Other times, researchers will use actual voters as quasi-experimental subjects by exposing a randomly chosen group of voters to some experimental treatment and comparing them to another randomly chosen group of voters not exposed to that treatment. For instance, Gerber, Karlan, and Bergan (2009) randomly assigned groups of voters to receive a free subscription of the *Washington Post*, a *Washington Times* free subscription, or no subscription at all to study the effect that exposure to a newspaper might have on political knowledge, public opinion, and voter turnout.

CHOOSING AN EXPERIMENTAL APPROACH

For the purposes of our study, we believe an experimental design offers the best approach.[1] Such a design allows us to control the ballot language, the use of provisional ballots, and the length of wait times at the polling place. Most importantly, an experimental approach allows us to observe the actual vote choices made by those casting ballots, which is something we cannot do in actual elections. An experimental design allows us go into the (mock) voting booth to see the actual ballot choices of those participating in an election, albeit an artificial one. We are also able to ask voters questions before they enter the voting booth to both assess their policy preferences and to randomly assign voters to different treatments at the polls. Finally, we are able to gauge the degree of stress voters experienced in reaction to such treatments. In short, an experimental approach allows us to observe and manipulate our subjects in ways that a field study, non- or quasi-experimental, would not.

Researchers laud experiments for their strengths in a number of areas. First, they allow for control, which enabled us to create a mock voting situation in a laboratory setting where we controlled for important extraneous factors that might affect voters in the field. For example, we made certain that no mock voters in our study passed by any campaign signs related to any of the ballot issues on which they would be voting on their way to the polling place, which is something we could not have done in a live election. Second, experiments allow for the random assignment of participants to different treatments so that we can be more certain that any differences in behavior result from differences in the factor under investigation rather than characteristics of the individuals themselves. For instance, we randomly chose who was asked to vote provisionally. If we observe that provisional voters tended to vote more inconsistently, we can be more certain that the use of a provisional ballot rather than voter characteristics, such as race or residential mobility (both of which have been associated with provisional ballot use in recent elections), caused the voting behavior. Third, experiments increase the degree of confidence we can have in cause-effect relationships; that is, they reduce threats to internal validity. If we posit that complicated wording on ballots causes voters to cast ballots that contradict their previously stated preferences, we must be sure that nothing else could be causing the incongruent vote. An experimental design allows us to control for other potentially confounding influences. Fourth, experimental results tend to be highly reliable or replicable. Because we followed specific experimental procedures, other researchers can easily replicate our experiment and compare their results to ours.

While experimental research offers many advantages, there are a number of disadvantages to this approach as well. Chief among them are concerns about the generalizability of the results, or external validity. Both the sample of subjects and their experiences often come into question, and our study is no exception. Like ours, many experiments rely on small samples of college students. In an attempt to better simulate the general electorate, we attempted to find a diverse set of study participants, and to draw enough participation to escape the problem of extremely low numbers of cases. We conducted our study on the Sam Houston State University (SHSU) campus and recruited participants of all majors. SHSU is typical of many state universities in the nation. It is a large public university located seventy miles north of Houston in Huntsville, Texas, and draws students mostly from the rural areas of East Texas and the Houston and Dallas metropolitan areas. The student body is racially/ethnically diverse with students generally coming from modest financial backgrounds, many representing the first in their family to attend college. According to the *SHSU Fall 2016 Institutional Handbook* (produced by the SHSU Office of Institutional Research and Assessment), the university had a Fall 2016 enrollment of 20,477 students, with a student population that was about two-thirds female and racially diverse. Just over half (52%) of students were Anglo, African American (17%) and Hispanic (22%) students constituted sizable minorities, and smaller proportions of Asian American (2.5%) and Native American (1%) students rounded out the student body.

Also, much like other experimental research, our study takes place in a "laboratory" (i.e., non-field) setting. To address concerns related to the artificiality that experiments bring with them, we worked to make our mock election more realistic. We required participants to register as mock voters in advance of the election, asking them to produce evidence of their registration at the time they voted. We set polling places that, like real polling places, experienced peak voting times when more voters arrived. Polling places were open before, during, and after class times, much like those in actual elections would be. Finally, we included language from actual elections on our mock ballot (discussed later in this chapter). Although no experiment can truly replicate the real election experience, we made every attempt to ensure that the mock election experience our subjects had was similar to one that an actual voter might have so that our results would be more readily comparable to actual elections.

EXPERIMENTAL DESIGN

To test our hypotheses, we conducted a two-stage, pretest/posttest experiment in the weeks leading up to the 2016 Texas presidential primary election in which we subjected participants in a mock election to several different polling place conditions believed to create a stressful voting experience. We recruited subjects from the student population of SHSU via posters, websites, class announcements, and email communication.[2] To encourage participation, participants were able to enter a drawing to win one of twenty $10 Starbucks gift cards for the completion of the pretest and one of fifteen $20 Starbucks gift cards for participation in the posttest, and some were given extra credit by their professors for participation in one or both parts of the study.

We asked participants to complete an online pretest survey about their voting habits and policy preferences prior to exposing them to an experimental treatment during the mock election.[3] The pretest contained measures of participants' policy preferences, political knowledge, media consumption, and party identification prior to the mock election experiment.[4] Upon completion of the pretest, we provided participants with the location and hours of mock election polling places and asked them to bring a registration confirmation code generated by the online survey with them to the polling place. In total, 605 participants completed the pretest (online) survey and 369 returned for the posttest (mock election). Only respondents who participated in both the pre- and posttest are included in the analyses presented here.[5]

Following the completion of the online survey period, we conducted a four-day mock election with polling places located in two different academic buildings on campus.[6] When subjects arrived at a mock polling location, a study administrator randomly assigned them to a treatment or control group.[7] Approximately one-third of the participants ($n = 122$) were asked to wait for a period of time (time recorded and varied for effect) before being given access to a computer terminal to begin casting their ballots, about another third (*n* = 120) were told that their eligibility as voters was uncertain and were given a paper "provisional" version of the ballot to complete outside of the computer polling station, and the remaining subjects (*n* = 127) were assigned to a control group and were led straight to a computer to begin voting immediately.

To increase the external validity of the study and add realism to the study, the mock election included races that were similar to the election that would occur during the upcoming Texas primary (held one week after the study was complete) as well as three different ballot referenda issues. Participants faced mock referenda issues on same-sex marriage, abortion access, and marijuana legalization. We chose to focus on these three social policy issues because these three issues were not being discussed extensively in any ongoing national or subnational elections in the state at the time, yet remained relevant to our study participants. All three represent "easy" issues. That is, symbolic issues dealing with desired policy outcomes that have long been on the political agenda about which people hold deep-seated, stable opinions. Such an issue "has become so ingrained over a long period of time that it structures voters' 'gut responses'" (Carmines and Stimson 1980: 78). Consequently, voting on such issues in a way that comports with their previously expressed opinions should present our subjects with an easy task. Thus, if we find that the subjects experiencing to more mock polling place stressors are less able to cast a posttest ballot supporting their pretest opinions, we can have more confidence that the stressful treatment played a part in their confusion.

While we mirrored the ballot language of actual ballot measures in other elections, these issues were not on the ballot in the 2016 Texas election. Consequently, these ballot measures did not receive much media coverage in local media markets during the 2016 primary election season. The dearth of media attention to these issues enabled us to manipulate the complexity of the ballot language in a way consistent with previous literature (Reilly and Richey 2011; Reilly 2010). Regardless of their experimental group, all participants received six ballot referenda, three with easy language complexity and three of more difficult complexity (Reilly 2010; Reilly and Richey 2011), that have a demonstrated effect on voters' ability to vote their preferences.

Sample Characteristics

Our study participants were between 19 and 50 years old, with an average age of about 21 (give or take about 3.6 years). Our sample reflects the diversity of the campus population. White subjects comprise less than half (45.5%) of our sample, while 19.5 percent of the study participants are African American, nearly 22.5 percent are Hispanic, close to 7 percent are Asian American, and about 2 percent are American Indian/Native American. As has become the norm, female students outnumber male students in both our sample (68.6%) and on campus (65%). Overall, our sample is likely to be younger than the general voting population of the United States but will be as, or more, racially and ethnically diverse than most college student samples. As indicated in Table 3.1, the subjects in our control and treatment groups have similar demographic profiles. Slightly older than traditional college students, our subjects range in age from 19 to 50, with an average age of about 21 years old (overall and within each group). Reflecting the campus population, our sample is comprised of about two-thirds women and one-third men, although the distribution of men and women differs slightly across the three groups. As expected, we have a racially/ethnically diverse set of participants, with a majority-minority sample in each group. Finally, our sample is overwhelmingly made up of US citizens but also contains a small number of others.[8] Taken together, the distribution of subjects indicates that we have three comparable groups of subjects when it comes to demographics.

Attitudinally and behaviorally, the subjects in our control and treatment groups also resemble one another. As shown in Table 3.2, a similar share of our participants consider themselves Democrats and Republicans, while fewer feel they are Independents.[9] Interestingly, a sizable share of our mock

Table 3.1   Demographics Characteristics of Sample, by Group

	Control Group (N=122)	Provisional Ballot Group (N=120)	Wait Time Group (N=127)
Age			
Mean (Std. Dev.)	21.3 (5.00)	20.7 (1.2)	21.1 (3.8)
Median	20	20	20
Range	19–50	19–31	19–49
Sex			
Male	22.8%	40.8%	31.1%
Female	77.2%	59.2%	68.9%
Race/Ethnicity			
White	42.5%	46.7%	47.5%
Black	19.7%	19.2%	19.7%
Hispanic	26.0%	20.8%	20.5%
Asian	4.7%	5.8%	9.8%
Unknown	7.1%	5.8%	2.5%
Citizenship			
US Citizen	89.0%	88.3%	86.9%
Non-resident Alien	7.1%	6.7%	9.8%
Naturalized Citizen	0.0%	2.5%	0.8%
Resident Alien	1.6%	0.8%	2.5%
Unknown	2.4%	1.7%	0.0%

Notes: All group differences are statistically insignificant at p<0.05 (two-tailed).

Table 3.2 Attitudinal and Behavioral Characteristics of Sample, by Group

	Control Group (N=122)	Provisional Ballot Group (N=120)	Wait Time Group (N=127)
Partisanship			
Democrat	39.4%	37.5%	36.1%
Independent	14.2%	10.0%	11.5%
Republican	28.3%	37.5%	33.6%
Don't Know/Other	18.1%	15.0%	18.8%
Ideology			
Liberal	42.5%	45.9%	42.6%
Moderate	4.7%	5.0%	3.3%
Conservative	52.7%	49.2%	53.2%
Political Interest			
Not at all	11.8%	15.8%	10.7%
Not very	22.0%	20.0%	24.6%
Somewhat	52.0%	46.7%	46.7%
Very	13.4%	16.7%	18.0%
No answer	0.8%	0.8%	0.0%
Political Knowledge			
Not at all	6.3%	7.5%	8.2%
Not very	27.6%	25.0%	25.4%
Somewhat	62.2%	59.2%	62.3%
Very	3.9%	8.3%	4.1%
Civics Quiz Score			
Mean (Std. Dev.)	73.1 (28.66)	75.7 (30.03)	73.4 (25.51)
Median	80.0	80.0	80.0
Range	0–100	0–100	0–100
Importance of Voting			
Not at all	6.3%	8.3%	5.7%
Just a little	17.3%	14.2%	10.7%
Somewhat	41.7%	41.7%	46.7%
Very	34.6%	35.8%	36.9%
Past Voting Frequency			
Never	81.9%	78.3%	82.0%
Once, the last election was my first time voting	9.4%	7.5%	7.4%
Twice	1.6%	6.7%	7.4%
More than two times, but I usually don't vote	1.6%	1.7%	0.8%
I voted in most elections	3.9%	3.3%	0.8%
I vote in every election	1.6%	2.5%	1.6%

Notes: All group differences are statistically insignificant at p<0.05 (two-tailed).

voters also report some other partisan identity or do not know what to call themselves. Anecdotally, many SHSU students express Libertarian leanings when polled on their policy stances. Importantly, however, this partisan distribution is comparable across our groups and somewhat comparable to the

US population, which is typically about one-third Democratic and one-third Republican. Ideologically, our sample also shows balance, with a roughly even split between liberals and conservatives and a smaller share of moderates. Again, the distribution across the groups is similar and somewhat reflective of the US electorate.

When it comes to how interested and knowledgeable our sample is, our groups also look alike. Regardless of their assigned group, our subjects tended to report a moderate degree of both. Although slightly more of the provisional ballot treatment group members reported being very knowledgeable about politics, their mean score on a six-question civics quiz shows no discernable difference in their ability to tell us what political office Joseph Biden held at the time, whose responsibility it is to determine the constitutionality of a law, the majority needed to override a presidential veto, the majority party in the U.S. House of Representatives, and which of the two major parties is more conservative. While subjects in the provisional ballot group scored about two points higher on the quiz, all the groups showed similar variation in scores and the same median score.

Our groups look most similar when it comes to their views on the importance of voting and their past voting behavior. Within each group, a number of our mock voters believed that voting is somewhat important, and a little more than one-third saw casting a ballot as very important. Since many of our subjects were too young to vote in the last election, a large majority of them (regardless of group) reported having never voted. Of those who had been to the voting booth in the past, the frequency of voting activity within each group was similarly distributed, although those receiving the provisional ballot treatment reported a slightly higher level of reliably voting in every election.

Measurement Strategies

We take as our dependent variable of interest each respondent's ability to vote in a way consistent with his/her preexisting policy preferences. On the pretest, all participants were asked to state, on a ten-point scale, their support for same-sex marriage, legalizing marijuana, and restricting access to abortion. At the time of the mock election (i.e., the posttest), respondents were asked to vote on ballot measures on these topics. As Table 3.3 illustrates, the distribution of responses we received from our subjects differed somewhat between the pretest and the posttest. Though our subjects, overall, reported stable preferences on the issue of abortion access, we see substantial numbers of our sample expressing different preferences when asked about their stands on same-sex marriage and legalized marijuana before the mock election and when faced with casting a mock ballot.

Table 3.3 Responses to Pretest Policy Questions and Posttest Ballot Measures

	Same-Sex Marriage	Abortion Access	Legalized Marijuana
Pretest Responses			
0–4	33.5%	34.0%	39.5%
	(122)	(125)	(145)
5	44.0%	10.9%	9.8%
	(38)	(40)	(36)
6–10	55.3%	55.1%	50.7%
	(204)	(203)	(186)
Posttest Responses (mock votes)			
No	43.5%	35.6%	25.2%
	(369)	(369)	(369)
Abstain	16.8%	9.5%	6.8%
	(369)	(369)	(369)
Yes	39.7%	54.8%	68.0%
	(369)	(369)	(369)

While more than half (55.3%) of our respondents reported generally supportive attitudes about same-sex marriage in their pretest survey, only about 40 percent voted in favor of the ballot measures allowing same-sex marriage in the posttest mock election. Support for legalized marijuana showed the opposite pattern, with support for legalized marijuana garnering about 17 percent more support in the mock election than on the pretest survey. While the relative distribution of responses to the question of abortion access remained fairly consistent between the pretest and posttest, some slight decrease in the share of subjects who opposed easing abortion access remains evident. These findings suggest conditions at the mock polling place might have led some subjects to cast ballots inadvertently contradicting their previously stated policy stances, but the numbers reported in this table do not allow us to examine which individuals, in particular, changed their positions. To better understand whether mock voters subjected to polling place stress were more likely to cast ballots in opposition to their earlier preferences, we need to compare each individual's pretest preference to his/her posttest mock vote. We can then test to see if those exposed to polling place stressors show a higher level of voting nonconformity than those who were not. Further, we can examine the associations that different forms of polling place stressors have with voting incongruities.

To do so, we created a vote conformity score for each respondent on each issue by comparing pretest preferences to posttest "votes" on the issues.[10] Participants who casted posttest ballots in a manner consistent with their pretest statement of preference were considered "conforming voters" and coded 1, while those who voted in a manner that differed from their pretest statement of preference were considered "nonconforming voters" and coded

0. We expected participants exposed to the voting place stressor of longer wait times to exhibit lower conformity scores, on average, than those who were not exposed to such stresses.

Voting can be a simple process. On Election Day, voters walk into their assigned precinct, go to a voting booth, and cast a ballot supporting the candidate or policy position they support. However, as we have already seen, not all voting decisions are equally complex. Some votes are simply easier to cast than others. Complicated ballots demand more cognitive processing than simpler ones, and direct democracy offers voters few cues on which to rely. Direct democracy elections, specifically initiatives and referendum, provide a question or passage for voters to read and vote on. These races require either advanced research and/or time to read and understand the proposition. Direct democracy measures are also highly sensitive to the environment (Nicholson 2003, 2005) and can be very complex for voters. Certainly, campaigns aid in the understanding and comprehension of these ballot measures; however, the language itself poses a challenge for voters, particularly when little information about such proposals is available. Thus, we strove to present our study subjects with mock ballot proposals that had not received much campaign or media attention and varied with regard to both topic and the complexity with which they were stated.

We measure ballot complexity using the well-established Flesch-Kincaid Grade Level index, which estimates the level of education required to read and comprehend a specific passage.[11] The Flesch-Kincaid index has been used in numerous circumstances as a measure of readability (Farr, Jenkins, and Paterson 1951), including assessing accessibility for Institutional Review Boards, newspapers, and other entities.[12] Further, the US Department of Defense utilizes the Flesch-Kincaid Grade Level test to measure the readability of official documentation to ensure users understand what they are filling out and signing. Specifically looking at political science literature, Magleby's (1984) research illustrated the connection between readability and participation on ballot measures. This was further examined by Reilly (2010) and Reilly and Richey (2010).

Our measurement strategies for provisional ballot use and length of wait at the polling place offered are more straightforward since we controlled both. We measure provisional ballot status as a simple dichotomy indicating whether the respondent was required to vote via a paper, provisional ballot (coded 1), or not (coded 0).[13] Our mock administrators challenged participants in the provisional ballot treatment of our experiment about their ability to participate in the same manner that a voter would on Election Day and required them to show multiple forms of state-issued photo identification. Those who were unable to provide adequate forms of identification (we asked for at least three) were told they would be able to participate provisionally, but we did not know if it would count (in the study or for extra credit).[14]

Approximately one-third of our subjects were asked to wait a period of time before they were allowed to enter the voting booth and cast their ballots via computer. We informed such subjects that there were no available voting stations in the room and asked them to take a seat outside the room containing the computerized voting booths. We did not offer them an estimate on how long their waits would be. We intentionally varied the amount of time the subjects in this treatment group were required to sit and wait, and while they were doing so, other mock voters were able to enter the polling station and vote without delay or were challenged about their right to participate. We coded whether a subject was made to wait (1) or not (0) as well as the length of time (in minutes) those who were made to wait did so.[15]

We viewed the reported stress experienced by the subjects during their participation in the mock election as an intervening variable. That is, we expected the ballot complexity, using a provisional ballot, and waiting before voting to subject mock voters to stress, and we expected that this stress would impair their cognitive capacities to a degree that they would be more likely to vote inconsistently with their previously stated policy preferences than those not experiencing such stressors. Consequently, we strove to measure stress levels at the time mock voters cast their ballots.

At the end of the mock ballot, we asked subjects to rate the degree to which sixteen different events occurred during the time they participated in the mock election.[16] Participants rated each event on an eight-point scale ranging from the event not occurring or occurring during the mock election but not being stressful (both coded "0" in this analysis) to the event causing him/her to panic (coded "6" in this analysis). We measure the overall individual stress level as the mean individual stress rating across the sixteen items.[17] Subjects reported overall stress levels ranging from 0 (30% of the sample) to 4.44.[18] As shown in Figure 3.1, those assigned to the wait time group reported the highest average level of stress and those randomly chosen to receive provisional ballots reported the lowest. This initial peek into the effects of polling place stressors suggests that worry over the use of provisional ballots might be somewhat misplaced.

ANALYTICAL TECHNIQUES

Throughout the chapters that follow, we conduct a number of different statistical analyses to test for relationships between different factors. Readers need not be well versed in statistical methods to appreciate our findings, but a basic understanding of the methods we use and what they

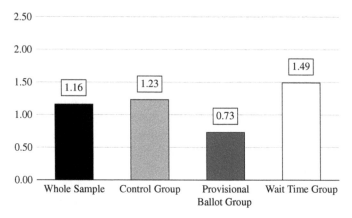

Figure 3.1   Mean Stress Levels.

tell us will likely help you appreciate what follows. Before proceeding to a brief primer on the four statistical methods we use throughout this book, we will share a short word about something called "statistical significance."

When we refer to findings as either statistically significant or not, we are indicating whether the results we see in our sample would be likely to occur in the population more generally. If a pattern of behavior we observe in our sample of subjects is statistically significant, this means that the same pattern would very likely result if we were able to study the population as a whole. We also often report the level of statistical significance, which offers some idea of just how certain we can be that the population would probably behave like our sample. Significance levels of 0.05 and 0.01 (noted as $p < 0.05$ and $p < 0.01$) indicate that there is about a 95 percent or 99 percent chance, respectively, that the sample looks like the population. So, the basic rule to remember is that a lower level of statistical significance (or lower p value) means more confidence in the result.

The first statistical method we frequently use, called an independent samples comparison of means test, compares the average score of different groups on a given characteristic. For instance, we could use such a test to compare the mean stress levels reported in Figure 3.1. Doing so would tell us that the difference between the average stress levels of those in the control group and those in the provisional ballot group is statistically significant at the 0.002 level. This suggests that if we examined the population as a whole, we could be about 99.8 percent certain that the same general pattern would arise. If we indicate that difference is statistically insignificant, we simply mean that we cannot be at least 95 percent certain that the same basic pattern would arise in the general population.

We also sometimes assess relationships between two variables using bivariate correlation coefficients. Correlation coefficients range from −1 to +1, with values closer to 0 indicating weaker relationships and those closer to either −1 or +1 indicating stronger relationships. Positive numbers indicate that as the value of one factor increased, it also increased for the other factor. For instance, we might study the relationship between age and stress level using a correlation. If our analysis revealed a correlation of +0.15, this would indicate that older voters report higher stress (and that younger voters reported lower stress). Conversely, negative coefficients indicate that higher values of one factor are associated with lower values of the other. So, if we saw a −0.15 correlation, it would suggest that older voters report less stress (and younger voters report more). In either case, the strength of relationship is the same, just in opposite directions.

So far we have only discussed investigating relationships between two different variables, but it is rarely the case, especially in politics, that something has only a single causal factor associated with it. Consequently, we also employ a multivariate analysis technique known as path analysis when investigating the effects of provisional ballots and wait times. Path analysis essentially gives us a way to estimate the effects that multiple factors have on an attitude or action. For instance, in chapter 5, we use path analysis to determine if the voting behavior of our subjects is likely to be related to provisional ballot use while simultaneously assessing whether the political knowledge level and voting experience of our subjects (along with many other things) contributed to the way they voted. Path analysis coefficients (also referred to as regression coefficients) can be interpreted like correlations, with the caveat that path analysis coefficients are not limited to a range of −1 to +1.

With these statistical tools in hand, you are now ready to dive into an empirical examination of the ways in which the use of ballot language, provisional ballots, and wait times at the polling place relate to voting behavior. Up first is ballot complexity. In the next chapter we use comparison of means tests and correlations to assess our subjects' reactions to ballot language. We test to see if our mock voters have more trouble casting ballots that align with their previously stated preferences when facing complex language.

NOTES

1. Special thanks to Dr. Richard N. Engstrom for his assistance with the experimental design, data collection, and coding of key variables.

2. See Appendix A for details about subject recruitment.

3. The online pretest survey was open to participants February 8–25, 2016.

4. See Appendix B for the pre-test survey instrument.

5. Independent samples comparison of means tests revealed no significant differences between the sample of pretest subjects who failed to complete the posttest and the sample who completed both waves on any of the demographic characteristics examined in Table 3.1 or attitudinal and behavioral characteristics reported in Table 3.2. The two samples show the same composition in terms of sex, age, racial/ethnic, and citizenship status as the sample used in this study. Similarly, the pretest only sample distribution of partisanship, ideology, political interest, political knowledge (both self-reported and civics quiz), sentiments about the importance of voting, or past voting behavior was similar to the sample completing both waves.

6. The mock election was held between Monday, February 22 and Thursday, February 25, 2016, with both daytime and early evening polling hours. See Appendix C for the posttest mock ballot.

7. Graduate students employed by the SHSU Political Science Department, along with the primary researchers, served as mock election administrators. All administrators followed the same script when processing mock voters.

8. Though only American citizens may legally participate in US elections, we include all subjects in the analyses that follow. We also tested all models excluding subjects of unknown citizenship as well as resident and non-resident aliens. The results were unchanged with regard to the direction, magnitude, and statistical significance, but excluding these groups does lead to the loss of about 10 percent of our sample and limits our ability to test some of the hypotheses that follow.

9. We code leaning partisans as partisans. Independents are only those who do not feel closer to one party of the other.

10. The ten-point scale that appeared on the pretest was recoded to classify subjects rating their support for each issues between zero and four as expressing a preference to vote against the ballot issue that appeared on the post-test (mock election) ballot and those rating their support from six to ten as expressing a preference to vote for the ballot initiatives. Those indicting their support at the midpoint on the scale (five) were excluded from this analysis.

11. Initially these were capped at a 1–12 grade level; however more recent publications have looked at the scale beyond 12th grade to provide additional context of how complex these measures are (Reilly 2010; Reilly and Richey 2011; Kincaid et al 1975). The formula does not have an upper limit and allows grade levels that can be larger than high school completion in the United States.

12. Specifically the Harvard Law Review, Time Magazine, and Reader's Digest utilize this measure.

13. In the analyses presented in the following chapters, we include those who experienced a wait in the "no provisional ballot" group. Analyses conducted excluding the waiting group reveal the same results with regard to statistical significance and direction of all relationships.

14. Participants were told in the debriefing script about the ruse of identification and that their participation did count. They were included in the drawing for a gift card as well as for extra credit (per their instructor).

15. We again include the other treatment group (those made to vote provisionally) in the "no wait time" category. Analyses conducted excluding the provisional ballot group reveal the same results with regard to statistical significance and direction of all relationships.

16. See Appendix D for question wording, coding, and distribution of responses.

17. Cronbach's Alpha for the sixteen-point scale is 0.954, and factor analysis suggests only one factor loading for all items, though there was some variation in factor loadings across the items.

18. The observed values of the scale are truncated because subjects rated a number of the items as not occurring at all.

Chapter 4

Can You Read Me?

Ballot Access Complexity and Voter Behavior

"This is gibberish," said Kelli Campbell, trying to grasp Amendment 4 while wrapping up lunch with friends in Ybor City ... This looks like a lease agreement," said Ed Wilson, a barista at a University Mall-area coffee shop. . . . Most people aren't actually going to read this," said Soleil Paterson, a University of Tampa student. Even Rosen, the Stetson law student, was tested by the language" (Stockfisch 2012). Voters' ability to give meaningful input on policy issues and influence policy choices represents the crux of direct democracy. Voters need to be able to understand the ballot measures they weigh in on and express their true policy preferences by casting votes that accurately reflect their stances on the issues of the day. Unfortunately, voters frequently find themselves in something of an information void when it comes to voting on policy proposals. Policy referenda items often receive far less media attention than candidates running for office, leaving voters in search of valuable information on which to base their decisions.

Ballot language is often the only material voters are exposed to prior to marking their ballots on policy proposals (Harmon 2010; Reilly 2010; Reilly and Richey 2011; Reilly, Richey, and Taylor 2012). Voters rely on the passages provided on the ballot to make real, consequential votes that influence policy outcomes in their cities and states. Consequently, the quality of the information provided on the ballot is critical. While concerns about the accuracy and potential biases of the ballot language sometimes become important (Burnett and Kogan 2015; Elmendorf and Spencer 2014), the ability of voters to understand ballot passages stands as the underlying issue when it comes to ballot language. Voters do not necessarily need to understand the long-term consequences of a specific policy, but, rather, they simply need to comprehend the content of the ballot proposition itself. That is, in order to cast a meaningful vote that accurately reflects their stances on the issue at hand, voters need to understand the policy option on which they cast ballots.

BALLOT COMPLEXITY

A healthy body of research documents the effects ballot wording and formatting often exert on voters. Scholars highlight two key aspects regarding ballot propositions. First, ballot propositions bring attention to the ballot and can increase turnout, and, second, ballot propositions can confuse voters. It is the latter argument that we address in this book. Direct democracy measures have often been accused of obfuscating the ballot (Schmidt 1989; Magleby 1984; Lipow 1973; Pillsbury 1931). There have also been a number of studies on voters' participation involving these measures and what affects their ability and desire to participate (see Nicholson 2003, 2005; Bratton 2003). And there is some evidence that the presentation or "framing" of ballot measures can be manipulated to influence voter decision-making (Burnett and Kogan 2010; Hastings and Cann 2014).

Studies on the readability of direct democracy ballot propositions have focused on different aspects of the ability to understand the passage on the ballot. Magleby (1984) analyzed the length of questions and the possibility of voter fatigue when confronted with several lengthy ballot propositions in California. Evaluating ballot measure language using the Flesch-Kincaid index, he determined that language complexity influences participation. That is, voters tend to participate less on more complexly worded ballot measures. Others have investigated this possibility nationally to determine the effect of readability on participation (Reilly 2010; Reilly and Richey 2011). Reilly (2010) examined the readability of ballot questions both in a national analysis of the Flesch-Kincaid readability scores and with an experiment. Experimentally, voters confronted with more complex ballot language were less likely to participate in ballot questions than those presented with less complex ballot language. This is further supported by Reilly and Richey (2011), who found in a national study that more complex ballot language on state ballot propositions is associated with a higher level of ballot roll-off (casting of incomplete ballots). Overall, the quantitative research in this area suggests that ballot readability consistently affects voter participation.

Other research examines the question from a qualitative approach. By looking at how each ballot measure is presented or "framed," researchers have determined that the information presented on the ballot can be manipulated to influence vote choice on specific measures (Burnett and Kogan 2010; Hastings and Cann 2014). The strong effects from language manipulation on participant vote choice revealed by these studies further illustrate the ways in which ballot language can be paramount to the quality of the vote and the outcome of an election. There is also evidence that, during the translation process into minority languages, minor changes can affect the voting decisions of minority-language voters (Hopkins 2011; Reilly 2015).

Research on roll-off has also offered explanations about why voters do not respond to specific questions on the ballot. Discussing roll-off as a function of a lack of understanding and education, Wattenberg, McAllister, and Savanto (2000) argued that voters only vote on the questions that they can answer. Other scholars have determined that the socioeconomic background, particularly race, and education, influence voters' decisions to complete the ballot by voting on all races/issues (Barreto and Ramirez 2004; Branton 2003; Vanderleeuw and Engstrom 1987; Magleby 1984). Findings from these studies further emphasize the importance of ballot language.

Given the evidence that ballot language can influence voter participation and vote choice, petitioners and the secretary of state's offices (or another designated body) can propose or revise the ballot language. On a positive note, revisions such as this can ensure that voters encounter ballot language that reflects the true meaning of the measure. However, from a more negative perspective, this ballot language can also be revised to complicate the issue or intentionally manipulate voters. Regardless of intentions, complex ballot language can obscure the true meaning of a ballot measure and confuse voters. When this happens, voters will be more likely to cast ballots that are inconsistent with their policy preferences. States have attempted to regulate the process of ballot language but often fall back to the more vague terms like "clear" or "straightforward" rather than empirical measures for ballot language (Pleshberger 2017; Milita 2015). States have also attempted to address potential ballot language problems with laws that reduce the complexity of issues, require only one topic per ballot measure, limit the types of topics allowed as ballot measures, and limit the number of measures on each ballot (Milita 2015; Reilly 2010). Still, there is worry that some issues are so complex that it is difficult, if not impossible, to modify them to simple enough terms for voters to easily comprehend (Burnett, Garrett, and McCubbins 2010; Reilly 2010).[1] Consequently, ballot language continues to plague election outcomes.

Does Ballot Language Matter?

Still, the presentation of language on direct democracy propositions is paramount to voters' understanding of what they are voting on. Voters may not be familiar with the issue being presented and may rely solely on the ballot summary to make decisions (Harmon 2010; Reilly 2010; Reilly and Richey 2011; Reilly, Richey, and Taylor 2012). Ballot summaries that are complex and difficult to ascertain in a quick reading can affect voters' decisions at the ballot box (Burnett and Kogan 2015; Elmendorf and Spencer 2014). Consequently, election officials, as well as researchers in this area, have made efforts to address ballot readability concerns.

Public opinion researchers offer guidance about expectations when it comes to ballot readability. Since they have studied the wording of polling questions at length to determine the impact it can have on both respondent participation and on the quality of responses given, their findings can add to our understanding of ballot readability and its impacts. Research on public opinion polls demonstrates that even minor wording changes can result in changes in answers given by survey respondents (Rasinksi 1989; Kalton, Collins, and Brook 1978; Bishop, Tuchfarber, and Oldendick 1978; Gallup 1941). Question wording has proven to be particularly problematic when looking at questions where respondents express what have been termed nonattitudes (Gallup 1941). Nonattitudes refer to the tendency of poll respondents to offer answers to opinion questions even if they really do not hold them when queried by pollsters. Nonattitudes in public opinion polling are parallel to nonsalient ballot propositions in elections. In both cases, those providing responses (votes) do not have information on which to base a decision but express an opinion (or vote choice) anyway. Misunderstanding of polling questions can have a devastating impact on the prediction of election outcomes, but misunderstanding of a ballot proposition has even more important impacts on the laws made in many states. Thus, question wording, word choice, and complexity are likely to influence voting on ballot propositions as they do answers on public opinion polls.

Question length influences both the willingness of survey respondents to answer questions as well as the specificity of any answer provided (Laurent 1972; Herzog and Bachman 1981). Similarly, the average sentence length (ASL) can also influence voting behavior on ballot questions. Lengthy ballot questions may confuse voters or obfuscate the intent of the ballot measure. While ballot propositions are different from public opinion polling in the answers respondents provide, the length of the question certainly can impact whether voters will read the entire passage or if they will even participate in the measure. There are, however, ways to overcome the problems associated with question length. Topic (Groves, Presser, and Dipko 2004) and clarity (Subar et al. 2001) have assisted public opinion pollsters in making certain questions easier to answer. Similarly, salient issues, those which voters are aware of and are informed about, can offer voters additional information outside of the ballot booth, which provides the ability to overcome complexity and question length (Key 1964; Carmines and Stimson 1980). Unfortunately, voters oftentimes find ballot measures far from salient.

Therefore, when it comes to voting in direct democracy elections, researchers have shown that the complexity of ballot language exerts an effect on participation rates (Reilly and Richey 2011; Reilly 2010; Magleby 1984). Generally, the more complex ballot measures are, the less likely voters are to participate in these questions. For instance, Magleby's (1984) study of voter fatigue demonstrates that the roll-off from the top of the ballot races (president, governor, senator, etc.) to lower elections on the ballot (typically ballot measures) in California is associated with lengthy ballots. And this tendency is not unique to the United States. Cross-national research also demonstrates that ballot language, as well as position on the ballot, decreases participation on ballot measures (Reilly and Richey 2011; Reilly 2010). Additional research on roll-off has suggested that roll-off is a function of a lack of understanding and education, indicating that voters only vote on measures they understand (Wattenberg, McAllister, and Savanto 2000). Taken together, these findings suggest that ballot language complexity likely impacts both the willingness of voters to cast ballots and the direction of the votes they cast.

THEORETICAL EXPECTATIONS

We examine several interconnected relationships in this chapter to determine the effects of ballot language complexity on voter participation and voting conformity to confirm prior results (Magleby 1984; Reilly 2010; Reilly and Richey 2011) and to evaluate its impact under different circumstances. First, we examine the relationship between complexity and participation and propose that if ballots are complexly worded, voters will be less likely to cast a vote. Since voters are unwilling to vote on things they do not understand, more complex ballot language has been associated with participation decreases (Reilly 2010; Reilly and Richey 2011; Wattenberg, McAllister, and Savanto 2000). Further, if voters get lost in the language, it may create further angst about government and a corresponding tendency to abstain from participation in the governmental process. Thus, we expected our experimental results to confirm and expand the previous research findings (Magleby 1984; Reilly 2010; Reilly and Richey 2011; Milita 2015) regarding voting on ballot questions.

It follows that when voters understand the question being posed, they are more willing to participate. Connected to this argument is how voters cast votes when they do participate. Ballot language, particularly complex language, impacts voters' ability to align their policy preferences with their vote choices. Because they may not understand the question asked, we expected that voters would be more likely to vote inconsistently when weighing in on more complexly worded ballot measures than when they face more easily worded ballot questions (hypothesis 4). We draw on the arguments of Bowler and Donovan (1998) and Lupia (1994a, 1994b, 2001), explored in chapter 1, and apply them to the circumstance of ballot language complexity. This argues that, in a vacuum, voters who are relying on the ballot passage to determine their vote can accidentally vote against the preferences when faced with language that is more complex.

Further, as outlined in chapter 2, voters who encounter stress at the voting booth are more susceptible to poor decision-making that can result in inconsistent voting. Voters can encounter stress in various forms (poll administrators, ballot language, long lines, or even being challenged about their right to vote), and these stressors can influence voters' decision-making. In this chapter, we focus on ballot language to determine if voters confronted with complex ballot language make decisions that do not conform to their policy preferences. We believed that complicated ballot language may place voters who do not understand the passage under stress and that this increased anxiety would make them more susceptible to casting incongruent votes.

MEASURING BALLOT COMPLEXITY

Previous studies have used aggregate voter turnout statistics and/or self-reported survey data about vote choices to ascertain the impact that ballot language complexity might have on voting behavior. While informative, such studies have limitations that our experimental design can address. Examining the actual choices made in the voting booth stands paramount to our understanding of the ways in which ballot language might affect voters and, more generally, election outcomes. Existing studies have been unable to observe the behavior of voters as they mark their ballots. Although post-vote survey questioning can reveal voters' intended vote choices, researchers relying on such data have no way of knowing if these self-reported vote choices match the actual actions voters took when marking their ballots. If complex ballot language puts voters under stress that influences their decision-making capabilities, it is likely that self-reports of voting intentions will inaccurately measure the actual votes cast. After all, voters cannot report about mistakes they did not know they made. Our approach to the question, however, allows us to objectively measure actual vote choices and compare them to previously reported policy attitudes. Thus, our experimental design enables us to more precisely gauge the effects that provisional ballots may have on voter decision-making in the actual voting booth.

We take as our dependent variables of interest the actual voting choices selected by our mock voters as well as their ability to vote in a way consistent with their preexisting policy preferences. We first examine whether each of our subjects chose to cast a vote on each proposed amendment and, if so, whether he/she voted in favor of or in opposition to the ballot item. As described in the previous chapter, we code voters as either "conforming voters" or "nonconforming."

We measure ballot complexity using the well-established Flesch-Kincaid Grade Level index, which estimates the level of education required to read and comprehend a specific passage. This formal measure provides an objective measure of how readable a particular passage is to readers. The Flesch-Kincaid Grade Level estimate is calculated by taking the ASL and average number of syllables per word (ASW), according to this formula: "(.39 × ASL) + (11.8 × ASW)−15.59" (Kincaid et al. 1975). The resulting score is equivalent to the number of years of formal education in the United States needed to read the passage under analysis. So a score of five (5) means a fifth grader can read and understand the passage. Similarly, since high school education ends at the twelfth grade in the United States, a score of sixteen (16) would mean the completion of high school plus four years of college education (a total of sixteen years of formal education).

We present the ballot wording for our six mock referenda and the Flesch-Kincaid Grade Level Score for each in Table 4.1. We took the text of these amendments from actual ballot measures in different states[2] over a ten-year period, selecting the easiest and most difficult language on each issue.[3] With scores ranging between about ten and sixteen, the first three referenda represent our "easy language" ballot measures. The Flesch-Kincaid index estimates that, on average, a mock voter would need to have completed high school and begun college in order to understand the three easy ballot measures. Thus, these measures should have been readily accessible to most of the subjects in our sample of currently enrolled university students. In contrast, the last three ballot issues have much higher Flesch-Kincaid index scores. With complexity scores ranging between about forty-four and eighty-four, these measures required mock voters to possess a very high level of education in order to fully understand them. The Flesch-Kincaid index suggests an educational level of almost fifty-nine years to understand the average "difficult language" proposed amendment. It is unlikely that many in our sample, or even the general American population, would have been able to understand these ballot measures.

The difference between the less and more complex ballot language for some issues is greater than for others. As shown in Table 4.2, the abortion issue shows the largest difference between the simpler and more complex ballot language. While the easier to read version of the question is estimated to be comprehensible by someone with about an eighth grade education, the more difficult to understand ballot measure requires an astronomical sixty-nine years of formal education. The readability difference for the other two issues is comparable, but both versions of the marijuana legalization topic are more simply worded than the commensurate same-sex marriage measure.

Investigating Ballot Complexity, Stress, and Voter Behavior

To test the effects that ballot complexity might have on voting conformity, we first examine the reported stress levels of our mock voters as they face ballot language of differing complexity. We then turn to the question of whether complicated ballot language dampens the willingness of these voters

Table 4.1   Ballot Language Complexity

Ballot Language	Flesch-Kincaid Grade Level Score
Amendment No. 1: This proposed constitutional amendment provides that marriage may take place and may be valid under the laws of this state only between a man and a woman.The amendment also provides that a marriage in another state or foreign jurisdiction between persons of the same gender may not be recognized in this state and is void and unenforceable under the laws of this state.	16.25
Amendment No. 2: Do you want to ban a specific abortion procedure to be defined in law, except in cases where the life of the mother is in danger?	12.25
Amendment No. 3: Title: Bill allowing medical use of marijuana Summary: This bill would allow patients to use marijuana for certain medical purposes. A doctor must find that the patient has a debilitating medical condition that might benefit from marijuana. An eligible minor could use medical marijuana only under the consent and control of a parent. There would be limits on how much medical marijuana a patient could possess. Patients and their primary care-givers who comply with this law would not be guilty of a crime. The state would create a confidential registry of patients who may use medical marijuana. Non-medical use of marijuana would still be a crime.Should this initiative become law?	10.28
Amendment No. 4 Title: Domestic Partnerships Summary: Shall there be an amendment to the Texas Revised Statutes to authorize domestic partnerships, an in connection therewith, enacting the "Texas Domestic Partnership Benefits and Responsibilities Act" to extend to same-sex couples in a domestic partnership the benefits, protections, and responsibilities that are granted by Texas law to spouses, providing the conditions under which a license for a domestic partnership may be issued and the criteria under which a domestic partnership may be dissolved, making provisions for implementation of the Act, and providing that a domestic partnership is not a marriage, which consists of the union of one man and one woman?	48.42

Ballot Language	Flesch-Kincaid Grade Level Score
Amendment No. 5	83.97
Shall there be an amendment to the Texas Revised Statutes concerning the requirement that any woman who is considering an abortion give voluntary, informed consent prior to the abortion, and, in connection therewith, defining several pertinent terms so that "abortion" includes termination of a known pregnancy at any time after conception, specifying the information a physician must provide to insure that a woman's consent to an abortion is voluntary and informed, requiring a physician, except in emergency cases, to provide the specified information to the woman at least twenty-four hours prior to performing an abortion, requiring the department of public health and environment to provide specified informational materials for women who are considering abortions, establishing procedures for emergency situations, requiring physicians to annually report specified information, requiring the department of public health and environment to annually publish a compilation of the physicians' reports, and providing for the administration and enforcement of the amendment's provisions?	
Amendment No. 6	44.36
Title: Regulation of Marijuana	
Summary: Shall Titles 32, 40 and 43 of the Texas Revised Statutes be amended in order to allow and regulate the sale, use and possession of one ounce or less of marijuana by persons at least 21 years of age, impose licensing requirements on marijuana retailers and wholesalers, allow for the sale of marijuana by licensed marijuana retailers and wholesalers, impose taxes and restrictions on the wholesale and retail sale of marijuana, and to increase the criminal penalties for causing death or substantial bodily harm when driving while under the influence of drugs or alcohol?	

Table 4.2 Readability Differences

Amendments	Issue	Difficult Ballot Readability	Easy Ballot Readability	Difference
Amendment 4-Amendment 1	Same-Sex Marriage	48.42	16.25	32.17
Amendment 5-Amendment 2	Abortion Access	69.22	7.97	61.25
Amendment 6-Amendment 3	Marijuana Legalization	44.36	10.28	32.17

to complete a full ballot and their ability to vote in a way that conforms to their previously expressed preferences with independent samples comparison of means tests. We compare the mean roll-off and mean conformity levels of our subjects on the more simply worded ballot measures to their willingness to complete their ballots and ability to vote in a consistent manner when facing more complexly stated proposals. Similarly, we compare the levels of reported stress levels of mock voters of different types and their ability to vote in a conforming manner with similar statistical tests.

Provisional Ballots and Electoral Experience (Hypothesis 1)

We have argued that the difficulty our subjects were likely to feel when dealing with more ballot language would lead them to feel more stressed about being unable to clearly represent their policy preferences. To rate the degree to which our subjects felt unable to communicate their policy preferences, we asked subjects to rate, on a scale from 0 (did not occur or "was not stressful") to 6 ("caused me to panic"), the degree to which they "felt misunderstood" during their voting experience. As reflected by the lower mean stress levels reported by respondents when facing either the more or less complex ballot measures in Figure 4.1, most participants did not feel this was a substantial issue in the voting process. At the same time, however, participants exhibiting higher levels of voting consistency reported higher levels of stress, and this pattern holds for the ballot proposals stated in both the easier and more difficult ballot language. Looking first at the more simply worded ballot proposals, those who reported that being misunderstood caused them "much stress" voted consistently almost 87 percent of the time, while those who reported feeling no stress about being misunderstood voted in a way that supported their previously asserted policy preferences only about 64 percent of the time—about a 23 percentage point difference between the groups.

The difference in these two groups of voters is even larger when it comes to the more difficult to comprehend ballot measures. Those expressing the most stress over being misunderstood cast conforming ballots about 83 percent of the time on the more complexly worded amendment proposals, but those who did not fret about being misunderstood were only able to do so about half (51%) of the time, constituting a 32 percent conformity gap between the two groups of mock voters. Taken together, these findings suggest that spending more time or effort understanding and voting in a manner that supported previously stated policy stances caused more anxiety than not doing so. Importantly, the fact that the more difficult ballot items resulted in larger increases in anxiety than the easier ones lends credence to our argument that polling place barriers, which is ballot language complexity in this instance, can indeed place voters under stresses that might affect their voting behavior.

Ballot Complexity and Roll-off (Hypothesis 2)

Having established that complex ballot language can cause voter anxiety, we next compare participation rates on the easier and more difficult ballot questions in Figure 4.2. Across all three issues, our hypothesis received support.

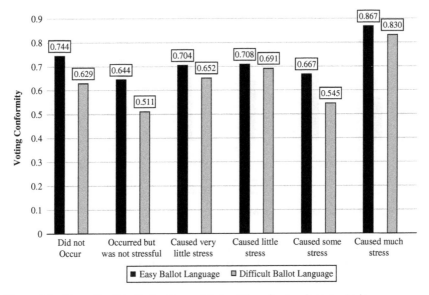

Figure 4.1 Mean Conformity by Stress of Being Misunderstood. *Notes:* Values are mean group conformity levels. Only one subject selected the highest, "caused me to panic" response option.

More participants opted not to cast a ballot when faced with the more difficult to comprehend ballot questions than when voting on the more easily worded ones. Further, voters were more likely to vote "no" when weighing in on the more complexly worded ballot. With the exception of the ballot measures on marijuana, our mock voters were more supportive of the more difficultly worded measures than the more easily stated measures. Our mock voters, overall, showed strong support for marijuana legalization, possibly because the age group highly represented in our sample tends to be more permissive about drug use and marijuana (Toch and Maguire 2014).

Ballot Complexity and Vote Conformity (Hypothesis 3)

Turning to voting conformity (consistency between policy preferences and vote choice) on the easy and difficult measures, the first row of Table 4.3 shows an overall difference of 0.10 in conformity when our experimental participants voted on measures stated more complexly than when they participated on more simply worded measures. When subjects read the more simply worded ballot measures, they were about 10 percent more likely to vote in a way that was consistent with their previously stated preferences than when they read and voted on the same issues stated in language that was more complex. Much the same can be said about the same-sex marriage and abortion access ballot proposals. On the same-sex marriage measure, mock

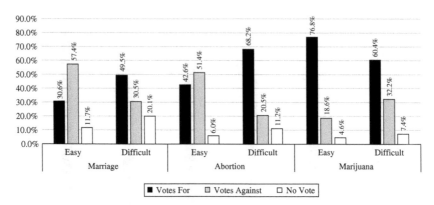

Figure 4.2   Vote Choice on Ballot Measures.

voters exhibited about 15 percent less voting conformity when weighing in on the more complexly worded measure. The findings for the abortion access proposal are even more impressive. When voting on the more difficult measure, our subjects were a whopping 39 percent less likely to vote in a manner that comported with their previously stated stance on this issue.

The opposite occurs, however, when looking at the marijuana legalization referendum. On this issue, our mock voters exhibited a 26 percent *better* level of voting consistency when facing the more challenging ballot wording. Given that the population of the experiment is mostly college students, this result may be a function of the topic (Toch and Maguire 2014). Additionally, there may also be some familiarity with the issue of marijuana legalization since several states have recently passed ballot measures on this issue, including the state of Colorado, which legalized recreational marijuana use. While same-sex marriage and abortion can be a more complex issues, voters, particularly young voters, are likely to view marijuana legalization as an "easy" issue to which they have a gut response (Carmines and Stimson 1980). Furthermore, the lower difference in readability between the easy and difficult ballot wording for the legalized marijuana issue than for the other two topics might also account for these unexpected findings. That is, our subjects simply might not have found the so-called difficult language regarding marijuana all that difficult. Altogether, though, these results offer support for our second hypothesis, along with an important caveat. While there seems to be a difference in how well voters are able to vote their preferences on ballot questions due to ballot complexity, it is important to remember that there can be issue effects and that not all topics should be treated the same.[4]

The Conditional Effects of Polling Place Waiting (Hypotheses 5 and 6)

Our results so far provide strong support for arguments that the complexity of ballot language can have a big impact on voters, especially on issues with

Table 4.3   Difference of Means: Conformity Scores on Easy and Difficult Measures

	Easy Ballot Language	Difficult Ballot Language	Difference	Significance
All Amendments (N=162)	0.73	0.63	−0.10	0.000
Same-Sex Marriage Referendum (N=236)	0.81	0.66	−0.15	0.000
Abortion Access Referendum (N=272)	0.79	0.40	−0.39	0.000
Legalized Marijuana Referendum (N=299)	0.57	0.83	+0.26	0.000

Notes: Cell entries are mean conformity scores for each group. Significance levels are from paired samples means tests. N=number of valid cases (listwise).

which they may be less familiar. We next turn our investigative energies to the question of whether some voters might experience the complicating effects of ballot complexity more acutely than others. Specifically, we investigate the possibilities that voter race, election administrator characteristics, and the predispositions that voters bring to the polling place may further amplify the problems that complicated ballot language causes for those looking to cast a ballot on Election Day.

We first examine the possibility that ballot language complexity might affect minority voters more than nonminority voters. Table 4.4 shows the average vote conformity levels for each racial/ethnic group on the easy and difficult worded ballot measures.[5] Almost all groups had high levels of conformity on the easy measures and lower levels of conformity on the more complex measures. The only caveat is the Asian group, which showed higher voting consistency on the more complexly worded measures. This group, however, showed much lower conformity across both formats of the referenda compared to the other racial/ethnic groups.[6] While the Asian segment of our mock electorate was able to conform about half the time to both the easier and more difficult ballot measures, most other participants were able to do so at least 60 percent of the time on the more complex measures and over 70 percent of the time on the simpler ballot items. The similarity between most racial/ethnic groups may be a result of our sample consisting of currently enrolled college students who have about the same educational level. Perhaps our minority subjects are relatively more educated than their non-college-attending peers in these racial/ethnic groups.

Table 4.4   Ballot Complexity and Voter Race/Ethnicity

	Easy Ballot Wording	Difficult Ballot Wording	Difference
White (N=77)	0.754 (0.238)	0.631 (0.238)	0.119
Black (N=25)	0.727 (0.285)	0.600 (0.254)	0.127
Hispanic (N=41)	0.741 (0.242)	0.667 (0.251)	0.074
Asian (N=9)	0.472 (0.264)	0.534 (0.290)	−0.062
American Indian (N=4)	0.833 (0.192)	0.319 (0.319)	0.083
Unknown (N=6)	0.583 (0.236)	0.417 (0.154)	0.166

Notes: Cell entries are mean group conformity levels (with standard errors in parentheses). N=number of valid cases (listwise).

We further explore the possibility that language minorities might face more difficulty when it comes to ballot language by using citizenship status as a crude measurement for minority language usage. Previous research suggests that minority-language voters have increased difficulty voting their policy preferences because of language barriers and translation issues (Reilly 2015).[7] As the conformity levels presented in Table 4.5 illustrate, across the board, most groups conformed less to the difficult measures than to the easy measures. Citizens and naturalized citizens (who have to pass an English proficiency test) performed better on both the measures with easier and more difficult language than their counterparts. This finding suggests that minority language use may indeed have an impact on conformity.

As a further confirmation that our mock voters perform in a manner similar to the general American electorate, we examined the voting consistency levels of men and women to determine if, as expected, our male and female participants behaved similarly. As Figure 4.3 shows, both men and women showed about 10 percent lower conformity on the more complex measures. While women, on average, exhibited slightly lower voting consistency on both types of referenda, there appears to be no meaningful difference in voting behavior between men and women.

Besides voter sex, research into voting behavior suggests that partisanship has consistently been a reliable guide to the voting preferences of Americans (see, e.g., Campbell et al. 1960). While ballot measures are nonpartisan elections, discussions surrounding them often take on partisan tones. Debates about topics such as same-sex marriage and abortion, in particular, have taken partisan language. Left without other information, voters facing ballot initiatives are likely to rely on their partisan instincts when casting their ballots. Consequently, it is essential to evaluate whether partisans are able to overcome ballot complexity to vote their policy preferences more readily than nonpartisans are. As shown in Table 4.6, the self-identified Republicans in our study demonstrated a better ability to navigate the more complex

Table 4.5   Voting Complexity and Citizenship Status

	Easy Ballot Wording	Difficult Ballot Wording	Difference
Native Born U.S. Citizen (N=146)	0.752 (0.242)	0.632 (0.245)	0.119
Naturalized Citizen (N=2)	1.00 (0.00)	0.889 (0.192)	0.127
Resident Alien (N=1)	0.889 (0.192)	0.667 (0.000)	0.074
Non-Resident Alien (N=10)	0.500 (0.192)	0.429 (0.242)	−0.062
Unknown (N=3)	0.444 (0.242)	0.667 (0.272)	0.166

Notes: Cell entries are mean group conformity levels (with standard errors in parentheses). N=number of valid cases (listwise).

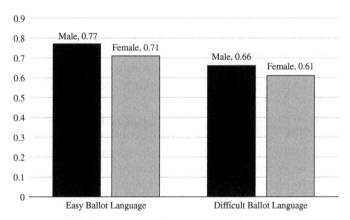

Figure 4.3   Ballot Complexity and Voter Sex. *Notes*: Values are mean group voting conformity level. ^p<0.10 (two-tailed independent samples comparison of means tests).

ballot language. The Republican segment of our mock electorate was only about a 1.2 percent less likely to vote consistently on the more difficult ballot items, while others showed declines of between 8 and almost 17 percent. Interestingly, the Democrats among our subject pool do not show the same tendency, nor do stronger partisans in general. Taken together, these results suggest that, as we hypothesized, the familiarity of issues to certain partisans can serve to ameliorate the challenges presented by complex ballot language.

In addition to partisanship, those members of the electorate who place a high value on voting as well as those who have experience casting ballots might be expected to better navigate complex ballot language. Those feeling that voting represents an important act are likely to be motivated to work more diligently to decipher confusing ballot language so that they can cast a meaningful vote. We asked our mock voters how important they felt voting was to them personally, and the voting conformity scores of those placing differing levels of importance on that act are shown in Table 4.7. Supporting our hypothesis, the results show that those who viewed voting as very

Table 4.6   Mean Conformity by Partisanship

	Democrat (N=62)	Republican (N=53)	Independent (N=27)	Don't Know (N=18)	Other (N=2)
Easy Ballot	0.741	0.714	0.700	0.783	0.500
Language	(0.254)	(0.221)	(0.332)	(0.238)	(0.333)
Difficult Ballot	0.572	0.702	0.595	0.652	0.417
Language	(0.250)	(0.224)	(0.262)	(0.262)	(0.167)
Difference (easy-difficult)	0.169	0.012	0.105	0.131	0.083

Notes: Cell entries are mean group conformity levels with standard deviations (in parentheses). N=number of valid cases (listwise).

important showed less than a 2 percent difference in their ability to vote in a consistent manner when facing more complexly and more easily worded ballot measures. In contrast, those feeling that voting was less important showed between 7 and 15 percent lower conformity scores on the more difficult ballot questions.

We might also expect that the more frequently one votes, the more likely he or she would be able to overcome ballot complexity. After all, those who have voted frequently in the past stand a better chance of having encountered such language before and being better prepared to confront it. We asked our mock voters how often in the past they had voted, and we examined conformity levels for groups of subjects with differing levels of voting experience. When looking at the differences in conformity between frequent and infrequent voters in Table 4.8, it appears that the frequency of voting may in some way help in overcoming the perils of ballot complexity, but perhaps not as much as many would expect. Both more-experienced and less-experienced mock voters exhibited conformity drops when casting ballots on ballot items stated in language that is more complex. At the same time, first-time voters and previous nonvoters appeared to have the most trouble with complicated ballot language, showing about 11 percent and 15 percent lower consistency on the more difficult items, respectively. In contrast, those who reported voting at least twice showed only about a 4.4 percent decrease in their ability to cast votes that accurately reflected their previously stated preferences.[8] Thus, as we predicted, participants with more voting experience are better able to overcome the barrier that complex ballot language presented.

Election Administrator Effects

The election administrator can also have a large impact on the stresses that voters face at the polling place and, consequently, on their ability to vote in a manner consistent with their policy preferences. Voter interactions with polling place workers have been shown to be capable of lowering voter efficacy

Table 4.7   Ballot Complexity and Perceived Importance of Voting

	Easy Ballot Wording	Difficult Ballot Wording	Difference
Not at all important (N=6)	0.788 (0.308)	0.714 (0.230)	0.074*
Just a little important (N=20)	0.767 (0.265)	0.617 (0.273)	0.150**
Somewhat important (N=64)	0.670 (0.278)	0.593 (0.239)	0.077*
Very important (N=72)	0.659 (0.215)	0.593 (0.239)	0.018**

Notes: Cell entries are mean group conformity levels with standard deviations (in parentheses). N=number of valid cases (listwise). $*p<0.10$; $**p<0.05$ (two-tailed comparison of means tests).

Table 4.8   Mean Conformity and Frequency of Vote

	Easy Ballot Wording	Difficult Ballot Wording	Difference
Never (N=124)	0.726 (0.250)	0.615 (0.248)	0.111***
Once (N=14)	0.800 (0.211)	0.646 (0.285)	0.154*
Twice (N=12)	0.711 (0.248)	0.667 (0.192)	0.044
More than twice, but usually don't vote (N=3)	0.222 (0.192)	0.333 (0.272)	−0.111
Most elections (N=7)	0.857 (0.262)	0.762 (0.252)	0.095
Every Election (N=2)	0.667 (0.333)	0.667 (0.000)	0.000

Notes: Cell entries are mean group conformity levels with standard deviations (in parentheses). N=number of valid cases (listwise). $*p<0.10$; $**p<0.05$; $***p<0.01$ (two-tailed comparison of means tests).

and trust in the voting process (Hall, Monson, and Patterson 2009). Negative experiences endured by voters even before they enter the voting booth might heighten their anxiety levels and lead to the types of limited and disorganized decision-making that has been shown by others up to this point. If this is the case, we would expect administrator characteristics to be associated with increased levels of reported stress and decreased voting conformity behavior among our experimental subjects.

To investigate the ways that a number of potential administrator characteristics might affect our mock voters, we employed five different mock election administrators with varied demographic characteristics, including diversity in age, sex, race/ethnicity, and regional residency. In total we had five different mock election administrators. Three were women, two were minorities, and two had Southern upbringings that might affect the perception of their demeanor when interacting with a heavily Southern mock electorate. This variation, coupled with the diversity of our subjects, allowed us to investigate potential effects that the race and sex of the election administrator might exert as well as the ways in which the demographic similarity between mock voter and administrator might affect the impact of ballot language complexity.

Table 4.9 Ballot Complexity and Election Administrator Characteristics

	Stress	Easy Ballot Wording			Difficult Ballot Wording		
		Marriage	Abortion	Marijuana	Marriage	Abortion	Marijuana
Hypothesis 5.2a							
Minority Administrator	1.16 (238)	0.87 (205)	0.77 (216)	0.57 (222)	0.62 (181)	0.37 (196)	0.88 (219)
Non-minority Administrator	1.15 (42)	0.79 (85)	0.81 (93)	0.57 (93)	0.67 (76)	0.43 (89)	0.80 (93)
Hypothesis 5.2b							
Same Race Administrator	1.13 (160)	0.81 (164)	0.83 (169)	0.60 (144)	0.65 (151)	0.37 (166)	0.85 (177)
Different Race Administrator	1.19 (160)	0.81 (130)	0.77 (145)	0.53 (146)	0.66 (113)	0.46 (134)	0.79 (146)
Hypothesis 5.2c							
Male Administrator	1.16 (117)	0.78 (97)	0.79 (106)	0.62 (108)	0.63 (88)	0.44 (97)	0.85 (111)
Female Administrator	1.15 (220)	0.82 (193)	0.81 (203)	0.55 (207)	0.67 (169)	0.40 (188)	0.81 (201)
Hypothesis 5.2d							
Southern Administrator	1.36 (95)	0.80 (84)	0.81 (86)	0.70** (89)	0.68 (74)	0.44 (77)	0.84 (89)
Non-Southern Administrator	1.08 (112)	0.82 (206)	0.80 (223)	0.52** (226)	0.64 (183)	0.40 (208)	0.82 (223)

Notes: Cell entries are the mean stress level reported on the 16-point stress scale, mean voting conformity levels, and valid number of cases, listwise (in parentheses). **p<0.05 (two-tailed paired samples comparison of means tests).

We first investigated the effect that minority administrators might have on raising stress levels and causing voters to be even less capable of understanding complex ballot language. As the first set of results presented in Table 4.9 indicates, there appears to be little difference in the overall reported stress levels of those who interacted with a minority administrator and those who did not. Similarly, few differences in voting conformity levels arise, although those facing minority administrators do appear to be somewhat less capable of casting consistent ballots on the more difficult same-sex marriage and abortion access proposals.

We next turn to the possibility that racial/ethnic congruence between voter and election official might serve to tamp down stress and allow voters to cast ballots in a more consistent manner. As the second set of results in Table 4.9 reveals, participants who interacted with a mock poll worker of a different race/ethnicity reported slightly higher levels of overall stress. At the same time, these subjects exhibited only slightly lower levels of voting conformity on half of the ballot proposals and not always on the more difficult ones.

Similar results emerge with regard to the sex of the election administrator (the third set of results in Table 4.9 shows much the same). Whether voters interacted with a male or female mock election administrator, they expressed the same levels of stress. Further, there appears to be very little difference in the conformity rates between those who dealt with a female rather than a male administrator.

Finally, we explored administrator demeanor and the familiarity that voters likely had with certain types of demeanor compared to others in the last set of results in Table 4.9, where we see slightly different, although somewhat counterintuitive, results. Contrary to our expectation, the mock voters working with a Southern administrator reported feeling more stressed. Interestingly, however, this increased stress level did not appear to hamper the ability of our subjects to cast ballots that reflected their policy preferences. In fact, those interacting with our Southern administrators were actually *more* likely to be able to do so on most of the ballot proposals.

DISCUSSION

Our results demonstrate support for several of our hypotheses. First, we found evidence that ballot language complexity did indeed cause our mock voters to express more stress about being misunderstood at the polling place. Experimental participants who indicated higher levels of being misunderstood showed less difference between their voting conformity on the more easily stated and the more difficult to comprehend ballot measures. Those who felt misunderstood seemingly made more of an effort to understand the measure prior to casting a ballot.

There is also evidence of increased voter roll-off when faced with more complex ballot questions. That is, our mock voters were less likely to vote on ballot measures with more complex language than they were when it came to the simpler ones. Third, our subjects exhibited lower conformity between indicated policy preferences and vote choice when confronted with complex ballot questions. Fourth, there is evidence that the topic addressed in the proposed amendment can influence voter ability to overcome complexity. When faced with a very familiar issue on which they likely held more stable and deeply held beliefs (legalized marijuana), our mock voters were better able to overcome complex ballot language and cast ballots consistent with their previously stated stances on the issue. Fifth, we saw that those viewing voting as more important had less difficulty with the complex ballot language. This finding suggests that electoral participants who highly value voting may make more effort to understand the measure prior to voting than those who do not value voting as much.

Also, as expected, voters who may be minority-language voters (using the crude measure of citizenship status) demonstrated decreased ability to conform their votes to policy preferences on complex ballot questions. However, there is no support that other voter characteristics (sex and partisanship) enabled participants to overcome issues of complexity (albeit this may be a reflection of the college-educated sample on which we relied).

In the final section, we evaluated some possible conditional effects that ballot complexity might have on voters' ability to conform their votes to their policy preferences. We discovered that the type of administrator generally does not appear to exert a strong influence on voters' ability to vote in a manner consistent with their preferences. Whether facing a female, minority, or Southern administrator, or an administrator of similar race/ethnicity, our mock voters showed fairly similar levels of voting conformity.

Overall, our analyses suggest that the complexity of ballot language presents a barrier to voters' attempts to vote in a manner consistent with their policy desires and that there are few differences in this effect for voters of different sorts. Given the strong effects with regard to ballot language and proposal topic revealed in this chapter, researchers would be well advised to keep both the complex language and proposal issue areas in mind when studying other possible polling place barriers. Failing to do so might mask important variations in voter attitudes and behavior. Consequently, as we turn our analytic attention to provisional ballot use in the next chapter and polling place wait times in the subsequent one, we will account for language complexity and issue domain.

NOTES

1. And, as some argue, if the issue cannot be simplified enough for voters perhaps it is inappropriate for voters to vote on these types of issues.

2. These measures are not all from Texas, but we adjusted the language to reflect that they were on the ballot in Texas to add realism to the mock election.

3. While our reliance on ballot language used in actual election helps increase the external validity of our study, it does present some measurement challenges. In particular, the ballot wording on some of the issues does not perfectly reflect the pretest measure of preferences. Thus, some might argue that subjects might be unable to vote their pretest preference since the ballot measure did not offer the same policy options. We feel this is precisely the task voters face in countless referenda elections across the nation, and is why we investigate ballot roll-off as well as vote choice. While we recognize the possible measurement error this might introduce, we feel the benefits of adding realism and external validity to the study outweigh the potential costs to measurement precision.

4. Paired (one sample) difference of means tests reveals the same results, both in magnitude and in statistical significance.

5. It is important to remember that these differences are somewhat muted because of the inclusion of the marijuana legalization referenda in the overall conformity score. The differences are much large when the referenda on that issue are excluded.

6. We observed that many of the Asian participants who participated in the process were foreign students. We address this issue in Table 4.5, where we use citizenship as a proxy for language skills.

7. While all participants attend or work at an English speaking university and participated in ballot measures written in English, the effects of unfamiliarity with the terminology could be more pronounced for minority language voters.

8. Since traditionally aged college students, many of whom were too young to have voted many previous elections, constituted much of our sample, those who reported voting twice are among our most experienced mock voters.

Chapter 5

Does a Placebo Ballot Lead to a Voting Headache?

Provisional Ballots and Voter Behavior

"Instead of a quick in-and-out vote, many California voters were handed the dreaded pink provisional ballot—which takes longer to fill out, longer for election officials to verify and which tends to leave voters wondering whether their votes will be counted" (*Los Angeles Times* 2016). "Phoenix resident Cecily Frutos needed to vote in the 2016 Presidential election before heading to her teaching job for the day, so she arrived at her polling place at 6:00 a.m. Despite her diligence, she was faced with a choice between completing a provisional ballot or not voting at all. Hesitantly, Frutos cast a provisional ballot and left for her classroom of students. Still, she was bothered by the fact that her vote may not have counted. 'I kept thinking about the last few elections in Arizona when the provisional ballot [*sic*] were not counted or miscounted for some reason from what I can remember,' she told a reporter when asked about her voting experience" (*Arizona Republic* 2016).

Since 2004, voters across the nation have faced similar decisions—vote provisionally or not vote at all—leading some to claim that casting a provisional ballot is "like voting, but it's not voting" at all (Palast and Bernstein 2016) and assert that a provisional ballot is nothing more than a "placebo ballot"—a false ballot that has no effect on the election. Even official government reports admit that, despite being cast by eligible voters, hundreds of thousands of provisional ballots were not counted in the 2004 election (Weiser 2006). And voters in some states have faced greater uncertainty than those in other states. Voters in Ohio, where more than 150,000 were handed provisional ballots that could have been nothing more than placebos (Liptak 2004), were especially likely to feel marginalized.

Following the 2004 election, then Ohio Secretary of State Kenneth Blackwell came under particularly intense media scrutiny for directing election officials in the state to count provisional ballots only if they were cast in the proper precinct instead of merely being cast in the proper county, as previously directed. To further complicate the situation, he had also reorganized precincts across the state, leading to high levels of voter confusion about their proper polling location. When a county election-board chair refused to implement the eleventh-hour edict, Blackwell threatened to remove him from the board (Hertsgaard 2005). Similar, though seemingly less egregious, reports emerged in subsequent elections in several states. A decade later, some were so skeptical of provisional ballots that they described them as "back-of-the-bus ballots" that were given to second-class citizens but not counted (Fitrakis 2014).

Still, not all Americans have had the same experience with provisional balloting. Studies show that provisional ballots cast in some states stand a much higher chance of being counted than in others. Alaska, for instance, counted over 95 percent of the provisional votes cast in the 2004 election, while Delaware accepted only 6 percent of the conditional ballots their citizens cast (Associated Press 2005). Following the 2008 election, there was evidence that certain states were consistently more likely to require provisional balloting and to treat such ballots as nothing more than placebos by rejecting them as invalid (Kimball and Foley 2009). Three states—Arizona, California, New York—and the District of Columbia, account for about two-thirds of all provisional ballots submitted across the nation and tend to lead the nation in rejecting provisional ballots. The US Election Assistance Commission argues that this seemingly persistent interstate disparity results from problems with the administration of provisional ballots and varied counting rules across the nation (Weiser 2006). Given the widely varying experiences voters across the nation have with provisional ballots, some might wonder why they exist at all. We turn to that question in the next section before moving on to our analysis of the potential effects such ballots might have on voter decision-making.

HELPING AMERICA VOTE WITH PROVISIONAL BALLOTS

Provisional ballots were enacted by the Help America Vote Act (HAVA) to ensure that eligible voters are not wrongfully excluded from voting (Ansolabehere 2007). The HAVA was enacted in 2002 following allegations of eligible voters being disenfranchised by erroneous administrative removal of their names from official voting lists during eligibility checks. In hopes of alleviating suspicions about the legitimacy of election outcomes, countering declining voter efficacy and trust in the electoral system, and adding greater protections for voters, Congress passed the law to create national standards and establish monitoring of challenged voting rights (see e.g., Fitzgerald 2005).

Critics voiced concerns that the greater availability of provisional ballots could add costs to an already expensive process and that the resources necessary to verify and adjudicate provisional ballots would take valuable resources from other, more important, areas of election administration. Further, some were worried that provisional balloting would allow ineligible voters to participate in US elections (Fitzgerald 2005), though this concern might be allayed by the fact that the addition of provisional voting methods does not appear to have affected participation rates across states (Fitzgerald 2005).

Diverging perspectives regarding the goals of provisional voting form the epicenter of the debate (see Foley 2004). Some view provisional voter laws as substantive changes to election administration, arguing that their use approximates same-day registration, which allows voters, pending no identification or registration form problems, to register at their poll location on Election Day. This view helps explain why states with same-day voter registration or those that do not require voter registration have been exempted from the law. Others, however, counter that provisional ballots represent no more than a procedural correction to an all-too-common election-administration error—the wrongful exclusion of properly registered voters. In the end, the act passed both the US House of Representatives and Senate by overwhelming majorities and was signed into law by President Bush on October 29, 2002.

The HAVA demanded states comply with minimum standards for voter and election protections through several provisions. The law required states to create an annual state reporting plan on changes to their voting processes. Voting systems and polling locations were required to be accessible to people with disabilities and computerized voter registration, voter identification requirements, and provisional voting were mandated. The law also created the Election Assistance Commission, which holds hearings and monitors state election activities. The HAVA further required that voters not found on the registration list, but who believed they had registered and were eligible to vote, be allowed to cast provisional ballots. Appropriate election authorities would subsequently determine these voters' eligibility and appropriately count or discard the vote.

Though the HAVA mandates that all states, except those with same-day or no voter registration requirements, offer provisional ballots to voters facing a variety of challenges, the act allows states a great deal of discretion when it comes to implementation. And disagreement about whether such voting should address a substantive or a procedural problem leads to many interstate (and sometimes intrastate) differences in application. Thirty-one states and the District of Columbia require voters to cast provisional ballots in the correct precinct, while fourteen others allow casting of provisional ballots in the correct jurisdiction—in the correct county even if in the wrong precinct, for instance. Further variation emerges in the ways voting officials may treat challenged voters. Some states have chosen to offer voters a ballot containing only races for federal office, while others allow provisional voters to complete a ballot with all races and ballot measures (referenda, amendments, etc.). In either case, election officials keep provisional ballots separate from the legal, unchallenged ballots that are cast. In most cases, challenges to voting rights are affirmatively resolved prior to deadlines set by the proper local official.[1] Such ballots get counted as full, legal ballots. Some provisional ballots, however, remain challenged and uncounted. Thus, voters asked to cast a provisional ballot may be offered assurances that, with more verification, their votes can and will be eventually counted, but they often still experience some doubt as to whether their ballot carries the same weight as those deposited in the official voting box on Election Day.

Voter Reaction to Provisional Ballots

While election administrators and the courts have spent a good deal of time deciding which voters should obtain a provisional ballot, which provisional ballots should be counted as valid votes, and where the authority for making such decisions lies, the ability of voters to cast ballots that will count is ultimately at stake. Given the limited number of elections in which provisional ballots have played a role, political scientists have only recently started studying the ways in which they might affect voters and election outcomes. Researchers do, however, point to three common themes when it comes to provisional ballots. They cite election administration errors as leading to a decline in voter confidence, point out potential partisan influences when it comes to verifying and counting provisional ballots, and highlight the differential effects that provisional ballots might have on different groups of voters.

Poll workers across the nation man the front lines of election administration, yet they are frequently undertrained when it comes to election procedures. Ambiguous state laws concerning provisional ballots coupled with decentralized election administration leave a high degree of discretion to poll workers when it comes to provisional ballot usage (Baybeck and Kimball 2008; Dao, Fessenden, and Zeller 2004; but see Liebschutz and Palazzolo 2005). Unfortunately, states often provide little clear guidance to these poll workers, leaving them at a loss when it comes to understanding when or how to issue provisional ballots (Alvarez and Hall 2006; Cobb and Hedges 2004; Kimball and Foley 2009). Consequently, questions about precinct jurisdictions, voter-identification requirements, and the proper criteria for voter-eligibility evaluations often flummox ground-level election administrators. And this confusion can adversely affect voters. Voter perception of poll workers has been shown to influence voter confidence in the election process (Hall,

Monson, and Patterson 2009). Confused or inconsistent poll workers may serve to undermine the legitimacy voters feel when casting ballots, especially provisional ballots. Voters facing the atypical act of casting a provisional ballot can have their fears about their vote not counting compounded by the attitudes and actions of undertrained poll workers.

Some argue such anxiety on the part of voters might be firmly grounded. When it comes to election engineering, states have adopted a variety of different practices. In particular, they diverge on the degree to which they verify provisional ballots—some states allow observers while others do not, and state law rarely addresses this issue (Foley 2008). This interstate variation opens the door to potential political maneuvering that can further undermine voter confidence. For instance, partisan effects have been found in the use and counting of provisional ballots (Kimball, Kropf, and Battles 2006). Provisional ballots in heavily partisan jurisdictions administered by an election authority of the same party are more likely to be cast and counted. If the precinct is strongly Republican and local election official is a Democrat, provisional votes are less likely to be cast and accepted (Kimball, Kropf, and Battles 2006). Thus, voters, especially those in certain precincts, may be even less confident that their votes will be accepted and counted as valid.

Finally, research suggests that certain voters may be particularly vulnerable when it comes to the use of provisional ballots. Traditionally disadvantaged voting groups as well as those who live in precincts with highly transient populations appear to stand a higher chance of being asked to cast a provisional ballot and having it rejected as invalid. Turning to the latter group first, voters who have recently moved must update their voter registration to reflect their new address. Problems can arise when a voter fails to do so or when official voter-registration roll books do not reflect a recent change. Researchers have shown a connection between higher levels of newly registered voters and higher usage of provisional ballots (Alvarez and Hall 2009). This evidence suggests that the process of moving can lead to questions about voter registration status, necessitating the use of a provisional ballot. Adding to the confusion, those who have recently moved likely have less familiarity with the voting locations in their new precincts and mistakenly attempt to cast a ballot at the wrong location. There is also some evidence that voters in large urban areas appear to be more commonly asked to cast provisional ballots (Kimball et al. 2006). In addition to typically having highly transient populations, large cities present voters with multiple voting precincts concentrated in small geographic areas. In combination, these factors can result in more frequent attempts to vote at incorrect precincts in large cities.

Turning to the former group, provisional ballots also appear to more greatly affect voters who have traditionally been at a disadvantage when it comes to voting. In particular, minority, low-income, and young voters appear to be more likely to be asked to complete a provisional ballot. Research has shown that provisional ballot use tends to be higher in more racially diverse precincts as well as in precincts with a higher percentage of population living in poverty and those in which a large number of college students reside (Alvarez and Hall 2009). Several explanations have been put forth to account for these patterns. The registration-cost argument posits that those possessing fewer resources with which to meet these costs of voter registration will be less likely to be properly registered. As a result, the same potential voters will be more likely to cast a provisional ballot. The costs of registering to vote include the time it takes to register, the knowledge of the registration process, and the money it takes to acquire any necessary identification. Just as those possessing less time, money, and civic skills will be less likely to politically participate in other ways (Brady, Verba, and Schlozman 1995), they are less likely to register to vote and to arrive at the correct polling place on Election Day. And lower income, minority, and younger individuals traditionally represent a large portion of the resource poor when it comes to political engagement. Younger people tend to register at lower rates and tend to remain registered at their home addresses while attending college (Bogard, Sheinheit, and Clarke 2008), and minority voters and the poor have been shown to be less likely to possess documentation to establish eligibility (Hood and Bullock 2008). Furthermore, because low income and minority voters tend to be concentrated in metropolitan precincts, they can also face the confusion associated with a multiplicity of geographically concentrated precincts, which has been shown to affect provisional ballot use (Baybeck and Kimball 2008). In fact, the racial effects of provisional ballots have been so pronounced that some have called them "second-class, back-of-the-bus ballots that are handed out freely in inner-city minority precincts and rarely counted" (Fitrakis 2014). We explore this possibility more deeply in chapter 7.

Taken together, aside from discussions about the legal ramifications and court challenges sparked by the HAVA, the literature tends to highlight various factors that influence the use of provisional ballots. There remains, however, the question of how provisional ballots might affect voters inside the voting booth. And it is to that inquiry that we turn our investigative lens, first discussing the reasons why provisional ballots might be expected to affect the actual vote choices made by those required to complete them.

The Stresses of Provisional Ballots

Despite a number of efforts to make the voting booth more accessible to the eligible public, getting registered and casting a valid vote can still subject potential voters to stress. The process of voter registration and election administration varies state by state, and even within a state, procedures for both often change. As reviewed above, such instability can cause mistakes on the part of voters and election administrators alike. Navigating such an ever-changing electoral landscape, confused would-be voters can easily find their voting rights questioned by election administrators. Confusion coupled with challenges to one's exercise of what many see as a fundamental American right, the right to vote, can lead to anger, anxiety, and agitation.

Reports of such emotional reactions have been readily forthcoming in recent elections. From coast to coast, voters asked to complete provisional ballots have expressed the same sentiment as a young Philadelphia voter who was informed that her registration had not been properly updated and that she would have to vote provisionally, "she filled out a provisional ballot and was angry to learn her vote would not be counted for at least a week" (Pompilio 2016). Even experienced voters can feel the frustration, as one longtime voter made to cast a provisional ballot told a nonpartisan organization in her city, "I am very angry over this situation" (Committee of Seventy 2012). Much of the anxiety seems to be rooted in skepticism about whether a provisional ballot will actually be counted (Lin 2016), but even those whose votes were deemed valid harbor resentment about their vote not being counted on Election Day. As some have observed, "Most people want their votes to count on Election Day. ... It's hard for people to feel their vote is important after they already know the outcome of the election" (Committee of Seventy 2012). In fact, the Pima County, Arizona, Recorder's Office has heard such complaints so often that they now include the following statement on their list of frequently asked questions about provisional ballots:[2]

> I am very embarrassed, frustrated and upset that my ballot did not count on election day and will not be counted until after the election is over.
> While this is not a question, it is a common expression received by the Recorder's Office. First, we are sorry that you are frustrated with the provisional ballot process or felt embarrassed in the polling place. The provisional ballot process is common and occurs in every election. The process is designed to ensure that you are given the opportunity to vote and have that vote counted if it is found to be valid.

Election officials issue provisional ballots only when a potential voter at a polling place does not seem to have complied with all requirements. Those issues are often deemed a function of the voter's error (e.g., going to the wrong location, filling out the registration form incorrectly, not having the correct form of identification), and the voter's alleged error is typically discussed and resolved in front of other voters and election administrators. Once a provisional ballot is deemed appropriate, the voter is made to vote in place and manner different from other voters. Thus, a kind of social stigma can result from being treated as a failure and being made to vote a "second-class ballot."

Voters describing themselves as embarrassed, frustrated, angry, and upset about being made to cast a provisional vote appear to experience a good deal of stress. While existing research demonstrates that negative emotional reactions to election procedures can affect voter confidence in the electoral process, we turn our attention to investigating whether this level of emotional upset changes the actual votes cast by provisional voters.

Investigating Provisional Ballots, Stress, and Voter Behavior

In this chapter, we focus on the potential stress caused by the use of provisional ballots, and attempt to discern whether voters made to cast such ballots are more likely to vote in a manner that is inconsistent with their previously expressed preferences. Using the measurement strategies outlined earlier, we assessed ballot roll-off by looking at the rate of nonparticipation on and support of each ballot measure. As in the previous chapter, participants who cast posttest ballots in a manner consistent with their pretest statement of preference were considered "conforming voters" and coded 1, while those who voted in a manner that differed from their pretest statement of preference were considered "nonconforming voters" and coded 0.

We measured provisional ballot use as a simple dichotomy and compared mock voters randomly assigned to the provisional ballot treatment group to those who completed a non-provisional ballot. In total, one-third (32.5 percent) of our subjects were asked to complete a provisional ballot. We attempted to make the use of this ballot more realistic by subjecting these mock voters to treatment similar to that faced by actual voters. Mock election administrators asked the subjects assigned to the provisional ballot treatment to produce multiple forms of identification, questioning the validity of each one until the mock voter could produce no more, and informing the voters that there was no a record of their registration to take part in the mock election. These subjects were then offered the opportunity to complete a provisional ballot and told that the vote they cast, as well as their eligibility for the gift-card drawing and any extra credit they were promised by their professors, *might* be counted, but that it would not be known until after their right to participate was fully verified. Those put through this treatment were visibly annoyed by the process, which was made all the more frustrating by the ability of other mock voters to proceed to the act of voting without such difficulty. In fact, one subject became very upset and combative, raising his voice while demanding to see the written policy that required him to have several forms of identification before storming off after being told there was nothing the administrator could do at the time.

In the end, however, all subjects offered the provisional ballot chose to complete it.

We first examined the impact that provisional ballot use might have on the willingness of voters to complete a full ballot and the ability to vote in a way that conforms to previously expressed preferences with an independent samples comparison of means test. We compared the mean roll-off and mean conformity levels of the control group with that of the provisional ballot treatment group. We then turned to multivariate analyses of provisional ballot use, stress, and voting behavior. We employed path analyses to test the effect that provisional ballot use has on voter stress and how such stress, in turn, impacts both roll-off and voting conformity. Following our general examination of the connections between provisional ballots and voter behavior, we turn to our hypotheses about the potential conditioning effects of administrator and subject characteristics.

Provisional Ballots and Electoral Experience (Hypothesis 1)

We first assessed subjects' feelings about their mock electoral experience. Since those subjects asked to vote provisionally experienced challenges to their voting rights were told their registration to participate was not properly filed, and they would, therefore, not be allowed to vote in the same manner as others, we expected provisional voters to report higher levels of stress related to these particular matters. We asked subjects to rate, on a scale from 0 ("did not occur" or "was not stressful") to 6 ("caused me to panic"), the degree to which each of the events shown in Figure 5.1 caused them stress during the time they stood in line to vote.

Since our subjects, on the whole, reported fairly low levels of stress, the overall stress levels reported here are not entirely surprising. The pattern of the results, however, does give us pause. Our mock provisional voters consistently reported significantly lower levels of stress related to each of the events. In fact, those challenged as to their voting eligibility reported that they were not stressed by any of the events. In comparison, the non-provisional voters reported that each event occurred but caused very little stress. Thus, our first hypothesis with regard to provisional ballots received little support. While many have argued that provisional ballots create a chaotic and embarrassing polling place experience for voters, our results suggest that even if this is the case, voters can readily weather the challenge.

Provisional Ballots and Ballot Roll-Off (Hypothesis 2)

Turning next to the question of whether those offered a provisional ballot were less likely to cast a complete ballot, we compared the participation rates of those casting provisional ballots to the participation rates of those casting

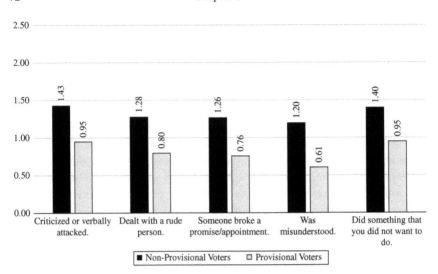

Figure 5.1   Reported Level of Stress Caused by Events at the Mock Polling Place. *Notes*: Values are mean reported stress levels. All differences are significant at p < 0.05 (two-tailed).

non-provisional ballots. Table 5.1 offers a first look at the differences in behavior between provisional and non-provisional voters. On the proposed amendments stated in either a simple or a complicated manner, provisional voters exhibited a stronger tendency to abstain from voting at all. While only about 1 percent of non-provisional voters failed to vote on a single amendment, regardless of ballot wording, almost 2 percent of provisional voters chose not to vote on the more easily worded measures and slightly more of them did so on the more difficultly worded proposals.

When examining a willingness to cast a vote in all three issue areas, this pattern persists, but only when mock voters faced more difficult-to-comprehend ballot language. While nearly 70 percent of non-provisional voters cast a valid vote on all three of the more difficult proposals, only about 63 percent of provisional voters did so. Interestingly, however, this trend reversed for the more simply worded amendments. Provisional voters appeared to be more likely than their non-provisional counterparts to cast valid votes on all three easier-to-understand proposals.

Taking a more nuanced look, when it comes to voting tendencies on ballot measures stated in more easily understood language, there is little difference in the nonparticipation rates or voting tendencies of provisional and non-provisional voters.[3] As Figure 5.2 suggests, about the same proportion of subjects, regardless of ballot type, chose not to cast a vote on the more easily worded same-sex marriage and legalized-marijuana amendment proposals.

Table 5.1   Voting on Ballot Measures

	Easy Ballot Wording		Difficult Ballot Wording	
	Non-Provisional	Provisional	Non-Provisional	Provisional
Voted on None	0.8%	1.7%	1.2%	2.5%
Voted on All	77.5%	82.5%	69.9%	63.3%

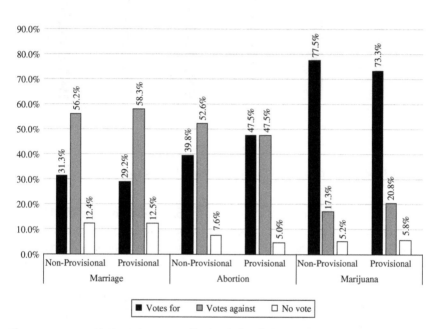

Figure 5.2   Vote Choice on More Easily Worded Ballot Questions.

And counter to our hypothesis, provisional voters actually seem slightly more inclined to cast a valid vote choice on the abortion-access proposal. Similarly, both provisional and non-provisional voters offer roughly equivalent levels of support for each ballot measure.[4] No matter whether a mock voter experienced a challenge to his or her right to vote or not, a majority voted against the same-sex marriage proposal, about half opposed freer access to abortion, and strong majorities supported legalizing marijuana.

Our hypothesis finds some support, however, when we examine the more difficultly worded questions (see Figure 5.3). In all three issue areas, mock voters made to vote provisionally showed a slightly stronger tendency to not cast a vote at all. While not rising to the level of statistical significance for the same-sex marriage and legalized-marijuana measures, the difference between the groups on the abortion-access proposal proved statistically significant ($p < .05$, two-tailed) and substantively impressive. While less than 10 percent

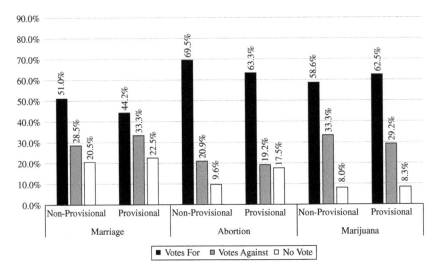

Figure 5.3 Vote Choice on More Difficultly Worded Ballot Questions.

of mock voters allowed to cast a traditional ballot did not vote on this proposed amendment, more than 17 percent of those made to vote provisionally did not vote a preference. This finding suggests that the combined stresses of difficult ballot language and provisional balloting might indeed be causing voters trouble in the ballot box.

When it comes to vote choice, the provisional and non-provisional mock voters again showed little difference on the legalized-marijuana question, with majorities of both groups voting in favor of the proposal. On the other two ballot measures, however, those voting provisionally showed a tendency to be less supportive. The same-sex marriage proposal won the support of a bare majority (51 percent) of non-provisional voters, but only about 44 percent of the provisional vote. At the same time, the abortion-access proposal garnered the support of nearly 70 percent of non-provisional voters but only about 63 percent of those who voted provisionally. Again, the combined stresses of provisional voting and difficult ballot language appeared to affect the voting behavior of our subjects.

Overall, our findings so far suggest that while provisional ballots might affect voting behavior somewhat, its impact may not be as strong as many have feared. There appear to be few differences in the voting tendencies of those made to cast provisional ballots and those allowed to cast non-provisional votes. Perhaps the use of provisional ballots has reduced tensions at the polling place. The combined effects of ballot language and provisional voting, however, appeared to vex our mock voters a good deal more when it comes to exercising their franchise.

Provisional Ballots and Vote Conformity (Hypothesis 3)

Moving beyond the choice to cast a vote at all, we begin our investigation into the ability of voters to cast a ballot that accurately reflects their previously expressed preferences by comparing the conformity scores of provisional and non-provisional voters. Counter to our hypothesis that provisional voters would be less likely to cast ballots consistent with their previously stated preferences, we found that such voters exhibit a higher rate of voting conformity than non-provisional voters (see Table 5.2). Taking all three of the more easily worded ballot measures together, our provisional mock voters were about 10 percent more likely to vote in a manner that conforms with their pre-election survey preference than those voting non-provisionally, though only the difference in conformity on the abortion-access proposal rose to traditional levels of statistical significance.

Similar results emerged with regard to the more complicated ballot issues (see Table 5.3). Though none of the group differences met traditional levels of statistical significance, provisional voters showed more consistency in voting the non-provisional portion of the mock electorate. Across all three issue areas, provisional voters were about 6 percent more likely to

Table 5.2   Conformity Scores by Group—Easy Ballot Language

	Control Group	Provisional Ballot	Difference	Significance
All Amendments	0.69 (143)	0.79 (81)	+0.10	0.006
Same-sex Marriage Referendum	0.79 (193)	0.86 (97)	+0.07	0.144
Abortion Referendum	0.77 (206)	0.86 (103)	+0.09	0.041
Marijuana Referendum	0.54 (211)	0.63 (104)	+0.09	0.109

Notes: Cell entries are mean conformity scores for each group and valid number of cases (in parentheses). Significance levels are from two-tailed independent samples means tests.

Table 5.3   Conformity Scores by Group—Difficult Ballot Language

	Control Group	Provisional Ballot	Difference	Significance
All Amendments	0.60 (122)	0.66 (63)	+0.06	0.189
Same-sex Marriage Referendum	0.65 (172)	0.67 (85)	+0.02	0.690
Abortion Referendum	0.41 (197)	0.42 (88)	+0.01	0.884
Marijuana Referendum	0.80 (207)	0.88 (105)	+0.08	0.066

Notes: Cell entries are mean conformity scores for each group and valid number of cases (in parentheses). Significance levels are from two-tailed independent samples means tests.

vote consistently than those voting non-provisionally. There was, however, some variation across the issue areas. On the marijuana-legalization issue, provisional voters seemed to have the largest advantage, with roughly an 8 percent higher chance of voting in a manner consistent with their previously stated policy position. In contrast, they were only about 1–2 percent more likely to vote consistently when it comes to same-sex marriage and abortion access.

Overall, then, it appears that provisional ballots presented little problem for our subjects. These results suggest that although many have derided their use, provisional ballots may not present much of a barrier to voters. It is also possible, however, that our provisional mock voters did not feel stressed by the treatment to which they were subjected in our experiment. Perhaps, as currently enrolled college students, our mock electorate consisted of voters who were accustomed to delays and questioning by authorities on campus and found the hassles they encountered in the mock polling place unobtrusive. To investigate the possibility that our provisional voting treatment failed to adequately stress our mock voters, we next tested the hypothetical linkages between provisional ballot use and stress, as well as voter stress and voting conformity. We proposed a causal flow, shown in Figure 5.4, from a set of exogenous variables (wait time, non-citizen status, and political knowledge) through an intervening variable (stress) to an outcome variable (voting conformity). That is, we tested whether provisional ballot use increases the stress our mock voters felt at the time they cast their ballots and whether that stress then caused their vote to diverge from their previously stated positions.

Since we have already seen that mock provisional voters do not show lower conformity levels than non-provisional voters, we have less confidence in our initial hypothesis. Still, it is important to control for other factors that might influence voter consistency as well as investigate the possibility that provisional ballots might put potential voters under additional stress, even if they did seem to cause our subjects to cast nonconforming votes. Given traditionally low rates of voter participation the United States, adding stress to an already unattractive activity may be something election administrators

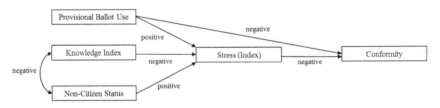

Figure 5.4 Hypothesized Relationships.

seek to avoid. Should we find that provisional ballots do increase the stress levels of our subjects, it might suggest certain reforms for provisional ballot use in US elections.

When it comes to factors other than provisional ballots that might affect the stress a voter feels on Election Day, as well as the factors that might influence a voter's ability to cast a ballot that accurately reflects his or her preferences, we would expect non-native citizens and those possessing less political knowledge to feel more stress than natural-born American citizens and those with more political knowledge.[5] Since those not born in the United States are not likely to have been socialized in the context of US elections, we expect them to feel uneasy when asked to act as a voter, even a mock one.[6] Similarly, we expect those with little political knowledge to be somewhat nervous about voting in an election they have been told will contain a number of important policy measures. And, of course, we expect those voting provisionally to experience more stress. Though we have already seen that provisional mock voters do not exhibit lower voting conformity, we will again test for a relationship between provisional ballot use and stress, while simultaneously allowing for the influence that any stress caused by provisional ballot use might have on voting consistency.

We employed a multivariate path analysis, predicting stress with wait time, political knowledge, and citizenship status in the first stage of the analysis. We viewed the reported stress, measured using the sixteen-point scale described in in chapter 3, experienced by the subjects during their participation in the mock election as an intervening variable. In the second stage of our analysis, we predicted conformity with stress, wait time, and controls for citizenship status, political knowledge, political interest, partisan strength, ideological strength, voting history, perceived importance of voting, age, race, ethnicity, and sex. We would expect those with less political knowledge and interest, weaker partisan and ideological commitments, weak voting histories, a perception of voting as less important, and those not born in the United States to be less likely to cast ballots conforming to their previously stated preferences. We believe that these voters will be less informed and committed to voting; thus, regardless of the polling place stresses experienced, we believe they will be less able to vote in a manner consistent with their previously stated preferences. While we are agnostic as to the relationships between the demographics of race, ethnicity, and sex, we believe that those who are younger may be less experienced voters and, consequently, be less able to vote in way that consistently reflects their previously stated preferences.[7]

As expected, the results, presented in Figures 5.5 and 5.6, support our contentions that those with more political knowledge report lower stress levels and that those with little experience navigating U.S.-style electoral processes (i.e., non-citizens) report feeling more stress.[8] Though not rising to traditional

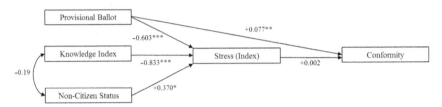

Figure 5.5⁺ Provisional Ballots, Stress, and Conformity—Easy Ballot Referenda. *Notes:* Coefficients are standardized betas from path analysis conduted with SPSS AMOS, Model predicting conformity includes the following control variables: political interest, knowledge index, non-citizen status, strong partisan dummy, strong ideologue dummy, past voting frequency, importance of voting, age (in years), African-American dummy, Hispanic dummy, and female dummy. *p<0.10; **p<0.05; ***p<0.01. ⁺Coefficients on all figures are unstandardized betas from path analysis conducted with SPSS AMOS.

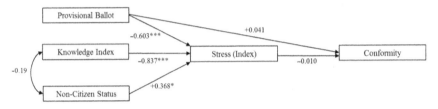

Figure 5.6 Wait Times, Stress, and Conformity—Difficult Ballot Referenda. *Notes:* Coefficients are standardized betas from path analysis conduted with SPSS AMOS, Model predicting conformity includes the following control variables: political interest, knowledge index, non-citizen status, strong partisan dummy, strong ideologue dummy, past voting frequency, importance of voting, age (in years), African-American dummy, Hispanic dummy, and female dummy. *p<0.10; **p<0.05; ***p<0.01.

levels of statistical significance, we also found support for our expectation that added polling place stress leads to lower voting consistency, but only when looking at the more difficult to understand measures. Conversely, higher stress levels are associated with higher levels of voting conformity among our mock voters. However, our earlier expectation that the use of provisional ballots places voters under stress or that their use is associated with the casting of nonconforming ballots finds no support. In fact, the use of a provisional ballot is associated with *decreases* in the reported stress levels of our subjects.⁹ And this finding holds when looking at either the more easily worded or more difficultly worded ballot referenda.

Substantively, these results suggest that when it comes to the ballot measures worded in easier to comprehend language, provisional mock voters reported a decrease of about 0.60, or about 3.8 percent lower, on the full stress scale relative to non-provisional voters. Similarly, provisional voters reported a decrease of about 0.84, or 5.3 percent lower, on the full stress scale relative to non-provisional voters. In other words, those hassled at the mock polling place and made to vote a provisional ballot reported feeling about 4–5 percent less stressed than those voting a non-provisional ballot.

Similar results emerge when examining the effects of provisional ballots and stress on conformity as they pertain to each issue considered separately. Turning first to the three ballot issues presented in simpler language, stress showed a negative relationship with voting conformity on the same-sex marriage and abortion-access measures (see Figures 5.7a and 5.7b). Though neither of the coefficients met traditional levels of statistical significance, these results provide some support for our hypothesis that increased polling place stress contributes to inconsistent voting. Counter to our expectation, subjects experiencing more stress appeared to be better able to cast a ballot consistent with their previously statement preference on the issue of legalized marijuana (see Figure 5.7c). Besides once again offering a perfect opportunity for a joke of the reader's choice about college students, stress, and marijuana use, this surprising finding corroborates previous research showing improved decision-making capabilities among high-level professionals facing stressful situations. "Overloaded executives" put under time

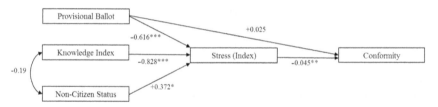

Figure 5.7a   Same-sex Marriage Referendum (Easy Ballot Language). *Notes:* Coefficients are standardized betas from path analysis conduted with SPSS AMOS, Model predicting conformity includes the following control variables: political interest, knowledge index, non-citizen status, strong partisan dummy, strong ideologue dummy, past voting frequency, importance of voting, age (in years), African-American dummy, Hispanic dummy, and female dummy. *p<0.10; **p<0.05; ***p<0.01.

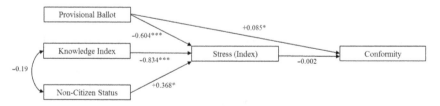

Figure 5.7b   Abortion Referendum (Easy Ballot Language). *Notes:* Coefficients are standardized betas from path analysis conduted with SPSS AMOS, Model predicting conformity includes the following control variables: political interest, knowledge index, noncitizen status, strong partisan dummy, strong ideologue dummy, past voting frequency, importance of voting, age (in years), African-American dummy, Hispanic dummy, and female dummy. *p<0.10; **p<0.05; ***p<0.01.

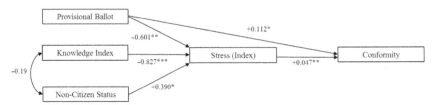

Figure 5.7c Marijuana Legalization Referendum (Easy Ballot Language). *Notes:* Coefficients are standardized betas from path analysis conduted with SPSS AMOS, Model predicting conformity includes the following control variables: political interest, knowledge index, non-citizen status, strong partisan dummy, strong ideologue dummy, past voting frequency, importance of voting, age (in years), African-American dummy, Hispanic dummy, and female dummy. *p<0.10; **p<0.05; ***p<0.01.

pressure in an experiment did, as predicted, narrow and limit the number of alternatives and amount of information they used to arrive at a decision. Interestingly, however, they were able to adapt their decision-making approach to rely on useful heuristics (mental shortcuts with which one is very familiar) to efficiently process information and make good decisions (Payne, Bettman, and Johnson 1988). Additionally, pilots exposed to "high workload pressures" in a flight simulator were able to make quality decisions under stressful conditions (Wickens 1996). Perhaps, like these executives and pilots, our mock voters employed a similar adaptive strategy that allowed them to "make the best decisions they can under difficult conditions" (Ganster 2005, 495), though only when it came to the easily worded ballot measure on legalized marijuana.

Unsurprisingly, considering the results of our earlier group comparison analyses, the results for the direct effects of provisional ballot use on voting consistency also largely contradicted our initial hypothesis. Ignoring statistical significance, those asked to complete a provisional ballot exhibited a better ability to cast a ballot that comports with their previously stated preferences on all three referenda.

The results for the more complex ballot language referenda offer inconsistent support (see Figures 5.8a, 5.8b, and 5.8c). Across all three issues, stress exhibits a negative association with voting conformity, though it is statistically insignificant with regard to all issues. Notwithstanding statistical significance, these coefficients suggest that mock voters reporting more stress and facing complexly worded ballots were less likely to cast votes consistent with their previously stated preferences. At the same time, the direct impact of provisional ballot use failed to meet traditional standards of statistical significance and showed a positive relationship with voting conformity on two of the three issues.[10] While those asked to cast a provisional ballot were less likely to cast ballots consistent with their previously expressed preferences

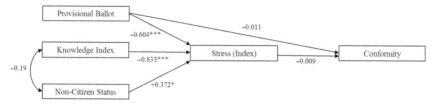

Figure 5.8a Same-Sex Marriage Referendum (Difficult Ballot Language). *Notes:* Coefficients are standardized betas from path analysis conduted with SPSS AMOS, Model predicting conformity includes the following control variables: political interest, knowledge index, non-citizen status, strong partisan dummy, strong ideologue dummy, past voting frequency, importance of voting, age (in years), African-American dummy, Hispanic dummy, and female dummy. *p<0.10; **p<0.05; ***p<0.01.

Figure 5.8b Abortion Referendum (Difficult Ballot Language). *Notes:* Coefficients are standardized betas from path analysis conduted with SPSS AMOS, Model predicting conformity includes the following control variables: political interest, knowledge index, noncitizen status, strong partisan dummy, strong ideologue dummy, past voting frequency, importance of voting, age (in years), African-American dummy, Hispanic dummy, and female dummy. *p<0.10; **p<0.05; ***p<0.01.

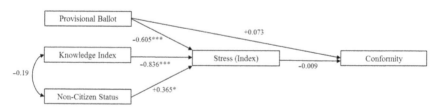

Figure 5.8c Marijuana Legalization Referendum (Difficult Ballot Language). *Notes:* Coefficients are standardized betas from path analysis conduted with SPSS AMOS, Model predicting conformity includes the following control variables: political interest, knowledge index, non-citizen status, strong partisan dummy, strong ideologue dummy, past voting frequency, importance of voting, age (in years), African-American dummy, Hispanic dummy, and female dummy. *p<0.10; **p<0.05; ***p<0.01.

about same-sex marriage, they were more likely to vote in line with their previously expressed preferences for the abortion-access and legalized-marijuana questions.

Taken together, the combined effects of provisional ballots and polling place stress ran counter to our initial expectations. Table 5.4 presents the

Table 5.4   Direct and Indirect Effects of Provisional Ballots on Voting Conformity

| | Easy Language Amendments | | | | Difficult Language Amendments | | | |
| | | Same-sex | | | | Same-sex | | |
	All Three	Marriage	Abortion	Marijuana	All Three	Marriage	Abortion	Marijuana
Direct effect	+0.142[a]	+0.030	+0.100	+0.105	+0.077	−0.011	+0.002	+0.089
Indirect effect	−0.002[a]	+0.033[b]	+0.002[a]	−0.027[b]	+0.012[a]	0.005[a]	+0.010[a]	+0.006[a]
Total effect	+0.140	+0.063	+0.102	+0.078	+0.089	−0.006	+0.012	+0.095

Notes: Direct effects estimated using the provisional-conformity standardized coefficient. Indirect effects estimated by taking the product of the provisional-stress and stress-conformity standardized coefficients. Total effects are the sum of these two estimates.

[a]single coefficient in path model significant.
[b]both coefficients in path model statistically significant.

standardized predicted direct and indirect effects of provisional ballots, with a value of zero indicating no impact and values of positive or negative one suggesting the strongest possible effect. Taking the more simply worded referenda issues, the combined effect of provisional ballot use directly on voting conformity along with the indirect effect of using such a ballot on stress levels, which in turn influences conformity, ranges from about +0.06 for conformity on the same-sex marriage issue to +0.10 on the question of abortion access, both of which indicate a weak effect.

The combined positive effects that provisional ballot use had on the more complexly worded referenda are similarly weak. The use of such ballots showed a standardized impact of less than +0.01 for the legalized marijuana referendum and an even weaker effect for the question of abortion access. Again, however, there was some variation across issues, with provisional-ballot use showing an even smaller, though negative, effect on conformity when it comes to the proposal on same-sex marriage.

DISCUSSION

Our expectation that provisional ballots would increase voter stress and lower voting conformity remains unsupported. Participants who received the provisional ballots reported less stress and exhibited higher levels of voting consistency. Further, the subjects in our study showed the same tendency on all proposed amendments, regardless of ballot-language complexity. Though potentially a nuisance, provisional voting appeared to help our mock voters cast ballots conforming to their previously stated preferences. Thus, while voters may be inconvenienced and slightly annoyed with provisional voting, their commitment to voting allowed them to overcome this potential barrier. While provisional ballots may still fundamentally challenge democratic representation in some ways, our mock voters appeared to be able to push through this potential barrier without much anxiety. While these findings run counter to our expectations, they do suggest that much of the angst surrounding provisional balloting may be much ado about nothing.

Looking beyond the effects of provisional ballots, the results of the multivariate regression analyses further suggest that some mock voters reported more stress and exhibited less voting conformity than others. Those who have less political knowledge expressed feeling more anxiety and appeared to vote less consistently with their previously stated preferences. At the same time, minority subjects, as well as those who were not born in the United States, showed lower levels of voting conformity. Similarly, those who view voting as more important and those with a richer history of electoral participation voted more consistently with respect to their pre-election preferences.

These results echo many of those from the previous chapter and suggest that certain segments of the electorate might be better able to overcome potential voting barriers than others. To further investigate this possibility, we analyze the dual influences of voter characteristics and provisional ballots in our penultimate chapter. In that chapter, we also examine the role that administrator characteristics might play in augmenting the effects of provisional ballots. Before turning to those matters, however, we look at the ways that long polling place wait times might affect voters in our next chapter.

NOTES

1. See the National Conference of State Legislatures website for state-by-state details: http://www.ncsl.org/research/elections-and-campaigns/provisional-ballots. aspx

2. Found here: https://www.recorder.pima.gov/faq_voter_provisional#j.

3. Independent samples comparison of means tests show no statistically significant differences in non-voting rates between the provisional and non-provisional ballots groups on the more simply worded ballot measures.

4. Again, independent samples comparison of means tests show no statistically significant differences in support rates between the provisional and non-provisional ballots groups on the more simply worded ballot measures.

5. Since our sample consisted of currently enrolled students, 12 percent of our sample were either current non-citizens or not native-born US citizens. We established citizenship status from registrar records, and considered respondents listed as aliens, naturalized citizens, or "unknown" to be "non-native." While we recognize that non-citizens cannot vote in U.S. elections, we felt that this subsample offers us the opportunity to investigate the possible effects of polling place conditions on newly immigrated, naturalized citizens.

6. Further, as students, our non-citizen subjects were likely aware that they do not have voting rights in this country. In fact, a number of our non-citizen subjects asked us specifically about this concern when they arrived at the mock polling location. Despite our assurances that they were not breaking any laws, may still expressed a degree of anxiety as they participated.

7. The deletion of insignificant control variables in the vote conformity models significantly reduces the fit between the model and the data. Consequently, the fuller models are presented here.

8. Also as expected, non-citizens exhibit significantly higher levels of stress and lower levels of voting conformity on all issues.

9. Full regression results are available from the authors upon request.

10. The same is not true of our non-citizen subjects, who report significantly more stress if asked to vote provisionally and lower voting conformity on the same-sex marriage and marijuana legalization measures.

Chapter 6

The Waiting is the Hardest Part?

Polling Place Wait Times and Voter Behavior

"[L]ines of voters snaked through and around the . . . building, all the way through the parking garage . . . as people waited as patiently as possible to cast their ballots" (Everhart 2016). "This is not what democracy is about" (Santos 2016). Recent presidential elections have sparked media reports highlighting long lines and voter frustration at polling places across the nation. The problems Ohio voters faced in the 2004 presidential election included seven- to ten-hour lines, sometimes in the rain (Dao, Fessenden, and Zeller 2004; Powell and Slevin 2004), something that some attempting to cast ballots in Florida during the 2008 election found themselves facing as well (Cohen 2012). And tens of thousands of Arizonans attempting to vote early for Trump or Clinton in 2016 found "all day, lines [that] meandered along church courtyards, zigzagged along school parking lots and snaked around shadeless blocks" (Santos 2016). It is little wonder why some voters might be driven away muttering in disgust, many without having cast a ballot. Long lines have been described as frustrating and potentially demobilizing by journalists, leading some to ask, "How many people decided not to vote because of long lines, and was it enough to make a difference?" (Dao, Fessenden, and Zeller 2004, 1). In answer to the first question, members of the US Congress estimated that five thousand to ten thousand voters in the 2004 election left their polling places out of frustration in the Columbus, Ohio, area alone and speculated that "many more never bothered to vote after they heard this because they had to take care of their families or they had a job or they were sick or their legs ached after waiting for hours" (*Congressional Record* 2005, S41).

WAITING AND VOTER TURNOUT

The commonsensical nature of the idea that longer wait times at polling places can deter some voters from casting a ballot makes asking why we might expect such a connection seem like an almost ludicrous exercise. It is important, however, that we do not blindly accept common wisdom in place of reasonably grounded theoretical arguments. We find at least two lines of reasoning that lead to the expectation of lower turnout in the face of longer wait times. The first stands on classical Downsian reasoning about the costs and benefits of voting, while the second finds its roots in consumer science research. Emphasizing that voting is not a cost-free endeavor, Downs (1957, 265) described time as the principal cost of voting. Time devoted to casting a ballot is time necessarily taken away from other demanding or preferential pursuits. Longer wait times drive up the costs of voting, which can lead voters to believe the benefits of doing so seem insignificant. Considering the potential benefits gained from casting an individual vote, someone who is asked to wait for hours in order to cast a ballot might find this expenditure of time too high a cost to pay when that same time could be spent completing an activity that offers more benefits. Working individuals might find earning another few hours' pay at their jobs more rewarding, parents might prefer playing with or caring for their children, and still others might fancy a trip to the multiplex to indulge in the latest Hollywood blockbuster. Time spent waiting in line to vote is time that could be used for beneficial pursuits, especially if, as Downs points out, it is unlikely that this individual's single vote will be the single vote that ultimately decides the election.

This same logic underlies arguments made by those working in the field of consumer science who study the ways in which waits for the delivery of service or products affect consumers. Researchers view waiting as a negative experience for consumers in both an economic and psychological sense (Piyush, Kalwani, and Dada 1997). Psychologically, they argue that a perceived loss of time due to waiting leads to stress and anxiety (a point to which we return later in this chapter); economically, they echo Downs's arguments about the scarcity of time. Some, in fact, take his argument even further, arguing that, unlike money, customers are *always* risk averse when it comes to time (Leclerc, Schmitt, and Dube 1995). That is, they will never want to spend more time on an endeavor, but might be willing to spend more money. They argue this attitude derives from the fact that time is less fungible than money. Losses or time cannot be as easily recouped or applied to other situations as money. For example, a monetary loss due to a meal costing more than expected might be recovered by spending less on snacks at the ballgame later, but a time loss of an hour waiting for the meal to be served is not as easily regained.

This mindset can be expected to lead to certain behavioral responses to waiting, including "balking"—not joining the wait line at all—or "reneging"—dropping out of the wait line after joining it (Piyush, Kalwani, and Dada 1997), both of which voters in recent elections have been reported to exhibit. Voters who arrived at their polling places and observed longs lines were reported to have left immediately, and some who became aware of the long waits at polling places before joining the lines were said to have simply not even gone to their polling place. The opportunity costs associated with forgoing other activities in order to vote have been used to explain both balking and reneging (Janakiraman, Meyer, and Hoch 2011). Devoting time to voting means giving up time spent on other pursuits and may lead potential voters to either fail to join a wait at the polls or to abandon such a line after joining it. Balking behavior is argued to occur, at least in part, because delays encountered very early in an attempt to achieve a goal are the most incapacitating. Early delays cause a psychological reaction that encourages disengagement from goal seeking (Lewin 1943). In other words, voters who knew they would face long waits to vote became less motivated to do so, regardless of the potential benefits. Reneging behavior, on the other hand, might be explained as a rational reaction to the perception that the costs of waiting in line increase the longer one spends doing so (Mandelbaum and Shimkin 2000; Shimkin and Manelbaum 2002). A voter who spends an hour in line may feel like it was time worthy of devoting to this task and not another, but a second hour of waiting may entail running late for or missing another, more beneficial engagement and prove to be too costly to bear.

Perhaps even more dire, some argue that consumers who feel dissatisfied after experiencing long wait times will be less likely to return to the place of service and more likely to communicate their dismal experience to other potential consumers (Carmon et al. 1995). Others find that a single such unpleasant experience can affect their overall judgments of the service provider and their subsequent actions (Anderson and Sullivan 1993; Boulding et al. 1993; Carmon and Kahneman 1993). These studies suggest that voters who committed to waiting in long polling place lines and were able to successfully cast ballots may still be less likely to return to vote in subsequent elections and will spread word of their negative experience to fellow members of the electorate.

EVIDENCE OF THE WAIT TIME–TURNOUT CONNECTION

The question of whether long waits at polling places lead to lower voter turnout has garnered its share of attention from academic investigators. Empirical researchers generally agree that substantially longer than average wait times at polling places can drive down turnout by about 3 to 5 percent, an amount that is likely to affect only the closest, most competitive elections. Taking the number of registrants per voting machine as a proxy for actual wait time, Highton (2006) finds only modest effects on turnout during Ohio's 2004 election. He argues that while long lines at polling places during the 2004 election might have cost Democratic candidate John Kerry some votes, it did not cost him the presidency. In raw number of voters, others estimate that a dearth of voting machine availability led between 18,500 and 23,445 voters to be turned away (Allen and Bernshteyn 2006). While this number of logistically disenfranchised voters can be argued to be a blight on the American electoral process, it amounts to less than 1 percent of the state's voters.

Studies examining the distance voters must travel in order to vote reveal a similar minor depressive effect on voter turnout. Gimpel and Schuknecht (2003) document the connection between the geographic accessibility of polling places and turnout. Voters who are estimated to have longer commutes to their polling places tend to vote at lower levels than those with more proximate access to a voting booth. They predicted that a five-mile increase in distance from the polling place would result in about a 2.3 percent decrease in turnout but note that this effect is not linear. In fact, those with excessively long commutes to their polling places exhibited higher turnout than those with shorter commutes. Haspel and Knotts (2005) corroborate the connection between turnout and distance between voters' residences and their polling places. They estimate about an 8 percent decrease in the probability of an individual casting a vote, especially if walking to the ballot box is not feasible. Similarly minor, though potentially important, decreases in voter participation have been documented outside the United States with simulated Canadian data showing that increasing the travel time to the polling place by about 30 to 45 minutes results in an estimated 2 percent drop in turnout (Blais and Young 1999).

Findings such as these have led some to argue that minimizing the costs associated with getting to the polls and casting a vote can increase turnout. Election Day vote centers, rather than precinct-based polling places, have been shown to boost turnout by about 2.6 percent (Stein and Vonnahme 2008), a level which effectively counters the turnout drop established by other studies. Proponents of Election Day vote centers argue that they help make voting less rivalrous and more complementary to the other activities vying for the time of potential voters. Voters may choose to vote at any vote center, and the centers are accessible throughout the day, so for example, a vote center located near a major shopping area allows an individual to cast a ballot and pick up groceries in the same commute, thus reducing the costs of voting by consolidating that act with another, necessary one. And since there are fewer vote centers than precinct-based polling centers, more voting machines and poll workers are likely to be available, which can help mitigate long lines and wait times.

Though the effects of wait times on turnout might be modest, there might still be important consequences for American electoral democracy. Beyond wait-induced turnout drops potentially affecting close elections, polling place wait times might produce important attitudinal effects that could affect subsequent elections. Scant evidence suggests that even though voters might commit to standing in lines in order to cast a vote, they express dissatisfaction with doing so (Conrad et al. 2009), especially when encountering waits that were longer than expected (Herrnson et al. 2013). Evaluations of both the overall service provided at polling places as well the poll workers in particular, have been shown to be modestly more negative when wait time is longer (Claasen et al. 2008) just as consumer research would suggest (Bateson and Hui 1987; Taylor 1994). Further, positive voting experiences have been shown to relate to factors such as poll worker quality and adequate voting machine allocation because both lead to lower wait times (Atkeson and Saunders 2007; Atkeson et al. 2010; Claassen et al. 2008, 2013; Hall, Monson, and Patterson 2009). Much like consumers who withstand costly delays in receiving products or services subsequently avoid and discourage further visits to the same establishment, voters who find enough benefit to voting to endure long wait times in one election, might abstain from succeeding elections and encourage others to do the same.

Overall, research seems to suggest that while long polling place wait times might exert some depressive effects on voter turnout, they are modest. Most who intend to vote manage to do so, even in the face of long lines. While about 2 to 3 percent of voters might be repulsed by the thought of waiting a long time to vote, 97 to 98 percent of those who intend to vote actually join the voting queue and persist until their ballots are cast. Still, it is difficult to understand how someone could bear to wait up to ten hours, often suffering uncomfortable accommodations and inclement weather, in order to cast a vote. After all, the benefits of casting a single vote in a presidential election would hardly seem to outweigh the costs such a wait would entail. Again, however, consumer science research may offer some guidance.

Some have argued that the importance of and proximity to the goal can play a role in explaining the public's willingness to withstand long waits. As Downs reminds us, the value a potential voter places on casting a ballot can increase the amount of time and effort he or she is willing to expend in pursuit of this goal. Similarly, market researchers have shown that customers will wait longer for a service they perceive to be more attractive (Hui, Thakor, and Gill 1998; Meyer 1994). Further, this research suggests that "there is a form of comfort in group waiting rather than waiting alone" (Maister 1985, 8). Recent presidential elections have activated the electorate in a way that other contemporary elections have not. The controversial 2000 election and subsequent Bush administration reactions to the terrorist attacks of September 11th mobilized the electorate on both sides of the partisan aisle. Voters heading to the polls in the 2004 Bush-Kerry race were likely more motivated than voters in previous elections to see their votes counted. Similarly, the historic candidacies of Barack Obama in 2008 and 2012, as well as the highly divisive and mobilizing 2016 Trump-Clinton race, drew voters to the polls with an invigorated energy to cast their votes in support of their preferred candidates. In addition to the added value voters likely attributed to their votes, those standing in long polling place lines in these elections could rely on the comforts afforded by their fellow balloters. Given the added perceived benefits of a single vote and the cost-reducing effects of waiting along with others, it is perhaps less surprising that most who sought to vote eventually did so despite potentially long delays.

It also appears that those who have devoted more time to a task might become more committed to achieving their goal. Time spent pursuing a goal can be viewed as a "sunk cost" that will be lost if the goal is not attained. As researchers in consumer behavior argued, when it appears "that the time and effort they have spent may be wasted, they should become more committed to the successful completion of the task regardless of the value of importance of the goal" (Hui, Thakor, and Gill 1998). And the anticipatory model argues that those who have invested more time in pursuing a goal will come to anticipate more highly the realization of that goal (Cahoon and Edmond 1980). Thus, voters who have waited longer might actually become more committed to casting a ballot and come to see their vote as even more valuable, both of which would boost the potential benefits of voting to a degree that they outweigh the costs of enduring a long wait.

THEORETICAL EXPECTATIONS

Even though most who set out to vote reach their goal of casting a ballot, it is still possible that long polling place wait times have some deleterious effects. Given the privacy of the voting act, researchers have focused on the question of whether long wait times repel votes and drive down turnout. We are more interested in exploring the possibility that those who endure long waits may be more likely to cast a ballot that runs counter to the expressed preferences. Perhaps those made to wait longer suffer some psychological stresses that cause them to make poorer decisions once they reach the voting booth. Existing research in the areas of psychology, political science, public administration, and consumer research offer some clues as to why this may be the case.

As we outlined in chapter 2, psychologists view stress as an environmental condition that affects people in most decision-making situations. Unavoidable and uncontrollable stressful contexts can place voters in situations that impair decision-making capabilities by causing them to limit their attention and ignore potentially important information. Subpar decisions often result because voters ignore relevant alternatives and process information in a disorganized manner.

As alluded to earlier, consumer science researchers see waiting as a negative psychological, as well as economic, experience. A typical waiting individual perceives a loss of time that causes stress and anxiety (Piyush, Kalwani, and Dada 1997). In fact, waiting causes "a broad range of unpleasant responses such as boredom, irritation, anxiety, tension, helplessness, and sometimes even humiliation" (Carmon et al. 1995, 1806), and it appears that these vexatious reactions increase the longer one waits (Osuna 1985; Palm 1953), especially when the duration of the wait is uncertain (Maister 1985; Osuna 1985). Some argue this reaction derives from the tendency to mentally concentrate on the opportunity costs of waiting (Janakiraman, Meyer, and Hoch 2011). That is, the longer a person waits, especially in a context when the expected wait is unknown, the more likely the individual is to start fretting about other ways the time spent waiting could be used. The stressful effects of waiting also tend to increase when no explanation about the cause of the wait is offered or others arriving later are immediately served (Maister 1985; Sasser, Olsen, and Waycoff 1979). So it appears that waiting may indeed be the "frustrating, demoralizing, agonizing, aggravating, annoying, time consuming" activity that FedEx told us about years ago (*Fortune* 1980, 10).

International relations and public administration scholars have added to these arguments in their examinations of elite decision-making. They argue that stressful foreign policy decisions often cause heads of state to shorten and narrow their perspective (George 1980; Holsti 1984; Sigelman and McNeil 1980). Similarly, Public Administration research has argued that the stress accompanying high-level job demands can lead top-level executives to make poor-quality decisions. As with political leaders, high-level professionals facing stressful contexts tend to narrow their perception, consider fewer choice alternatives, and/or consider fewer bits of evidence when evaluating different alternatives (Ganster 2005; Hambrick, Finkelstein, and Mooney 2005; Hammond 2000). In particular, time pressures and time spent in meetings instead of focusing on task completion, tend to drive up stress (Im 2009). Time and workload pressures have been shown to contribute to poor job performance and depressed creativity in professionals, diminished satisfaction, and worse health and well-being (Elsbach and Hargadon 2006; Ritti 1971; Robinson and Godbey 1998).

In our study, we investigated the possibility that waiting-induced stress might adversely affect the decision-making abilities of the mass public in ways similar to elite decision makers. As reviewed earlier, aggregate studies of voters' responses to national tragedies suggest that voters are indeed affected by these anxiety-filled events when they cast their ballots in subsequent elections (see, e.g., Ben-Erza et al 2013; Kaiser and Moore 2001; Sinclair et al. 2011). Further, a recent study of electronic voting technology suggests that voter performance in casting a ballot might become impaired under time pressures. "When there is pressure to be quick—for example because long lines of voters are waiting to take their turn or because the appearance of having trouble with the system humiliates the voter—some voters are likely to become flustered" (Conrad et al. 2009, 122).

Investigating Waiting, Stress, and Voter Behavior

Using the measurement strategies outlined earlier, we assess ballot roll-off by looking at the rate of nonparticipation in and support of each ballot measure. As in the previous chapters, we again code voters as either "conforming voters" or "nonconforming." We measure wait as the time (in minutes) that a subject was asked to wait. The mean wait time for this group was 10.84 minutes +/− 3.65 (SD), with about half (48.4 percent) of this treatment group experiencing a wait of 10 minutes or longer. Using existing research as a guide, we attempted to make the wait more stressful by not explaining the cause of the wait, allowing some mock voters arriving later to proceed to the voting booth unimpeded, and varying the duration of the wait without informing voters of how long it would be. Since many students were participating in the mock election between classes or other campus activities, we felt waits of this length would cause them to fret while not impeding their ability to attend to previously scheduled events. Anecdotal evidence suggests that the treatment worked. Consistent with research showing today's college-aged Millennial Generation to be impatient (Sweeney 2005, 2006; Ng, Schwiter, and Lyons 2010; Myers and Sadaghiani 2010; Hershatter and Epstien 2010), mock election administrators overheard a healthy number of waiting students complain about the wait and observed them repeatedly checking their watches and shifting in their seats, especially when we reprimanded them for excessively chatting with others in the waiting queue after seeing other mock voters walk directly into the voting station without a wait.

To test the effects that wait times might have on voting conformity, we first examined the impact that wait times at the polling place might have on the willingness of voters to complete a full ballot and their ability to vote in a way that conforms to previously expressed preferences with an independent samples comparison of means test. We investigated overall group conformity levels using an independent samples comparison of means test. We compared the mean conformity levels of the control group with that of the wait treatment group for each ballot referendum as well as the overall conformity levels of each group. We then turned to multivariate analyses of wait times, stress, and voting conformity. To better model our theoretical expectations, we employed a path analysis to test the effect that wait time has on voter stress and how such stress, in turn, relates to voting conformity. Following our general examination of the connections between wait times and voter behavior, we turned to our specific hypotheses about the potential conditioning effects of administrator and subject characteristics.

Waiting and Electoral Experience (Hypothesis 1)

We first assessed subjects' feelings about their mock electoral experience. Because we did not offer those subjects asked to wait an explanation as to why they would have to do so or how long the wait would be, and they witnessed others proceeding to the voting booth without first waiting, we expected voters made to wait to report higher levels of stress related to these particular matters. We asked subjects to rate, on a scale from 0 (did not occur or "was not stressful") to 6 ("caused me to panic"), the degree to which each of the events shown in Figure 6.1 affected them during the time they stood in line to vote.

Though the overall low level of stress reported by our subjects here is reflective of the fact that all mock voters, whether made to wait or not, reported low levels of stress, the results confirm our suspicions. Those asked to wait reported feeling more stress about having a promise broken, dealing with a rude person, and doing something they did not want to do. These subjects were much more likely to enter the voting booth irritated by their interactions with the election officials. Mock voters experiencing a wait also reported higher levels of stress related to matters associated with spending time on a wait of indeterminate length for unknown causes. Those who waited reported significantly higher levels of stress related to waiting longer than they wanted and having someone "cut" in line in front of them as well as hurrying to meet a deadline. These findings provide support for our first hypothesis with regard to the impact that polling place wait has on voters. Subjects experiencing a wait reported higher levels of stress related to the act of waiting that they carried with them into the voting booth.

Waiting and Ballot Roll-Off (Hypothesis 2)

Turning next to the question of whether or not those made to wait are less likely to cast a complete ballot, we compared the participation rate of those experiencing a wait at the mock polling place to that of mock voters allowed

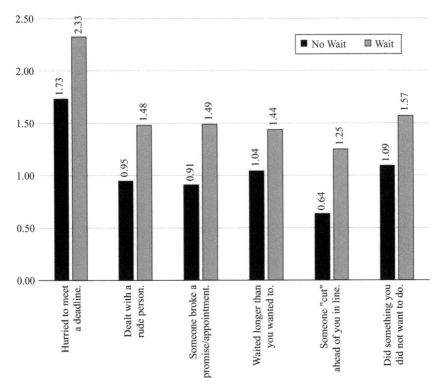

Figure 6.1   Reported Level of Stress Caused by Events at the Mock Polling Place. *Notes:* Values are mean reported stress levels. All differences are significant at p < 0.05 (two-tailed).

to vote without a wait. Table 6.1 offers a first look at the behavior of the two groups. On the proposed amendments stated in easier ballot language, mock voters made to wait showed a stronger tendency to abstain from voting at all. While less than 1 percent of non-waiting voters failed to vote on a single easily worded amendment, 1.6 percent of voters experiencing a wait did so. Both groups, however, failed to vote on any of the more difficult to understand amendments at the same rate. In fact, the more difficult language seemed to give those in the non-waiting group relatively more trouble. While mock voters allowed to proceed to voting without a delay showed a ballot roll-off rate twice as high when facing the tougher ballot language, those made to wait showed the same rate of roll-off for both sets of amendments.

When examining the willingness to cast a vote in all three issue areas, a different pattern emerged. Those made to wait exhibited slightly higher levels of ballot completion than their non-waiting counterparts, and this pattern held when we investigated the rates of casting a valid vote on only one or two

Table 6.1 Voting on Ballot Measures

	Easy Ballot Wording		Difficult Ballot Wording	
	No Wait	Wait	No Wait	Wait
Voted on None	0.8%	1.6%	1.6%	1.6%
Voted on All	78.9%	79.5%	66.8%	69.7%

of the amendments in each ballot language category. Taken together, these results suggest that voters experiencing waits at the polling place may actually become more committed to completing their ballots.

A closer look at voting tendencies reveals that mock voters who waited before voting were much more likely to fail to cast a vote on the easily worded abortion access referendum (see Figure 6.1). Nearly 10 percent of those made to wait did not cast a preference vote on this measure, but only about 5 percent of the non-waiting voters failed to vote on that issue. In contrast, about 5 percent both groups failed to vote on the legalized marijuana ballot item, and more of the non-waiting group refrained from voting a preference on the same-sex marriage matter.[1] When it comes to vote preference, both waiting and non-waiting voters offered roughly equivalent levels of support for each ballot measure.[2] No matter whether a mock voter experienced a wait before voting or not, a majority voted against the same-sex marriage proposal, about half opposed freer access to abortion, and strong majorities supported legalizing marijuana.

Our hypothesis found even less support when we observed voting tendencies on the more difficultly worded questions (see Figure 6.2). About one-fifth of voters—waiting and non-waiting voters alike—failed to cast a vote on the more difficult to comprehend same-sex marriage ballot item. And, in contradiction to our hypothesis, voters made to wait showed less of a tendency to roll off of the abortion access and legalized marijuana amendments.

When it comes to vote choice, however, non-waiting voters showed a slightly stronger tendency to vote against the more complexly worded amendments in all three issue areas. Roughly 1 percent more of the non-waiting mock voters opposed the same-sex marriage and legalized marijuana proposals, and about 3 percent more of this group opposed the abortion access amendment. Though not rising to traditional levels of statistical significance, these results do suggest that waiting may have some minor impact on voter behavior.

Overall, our findings so far suggest that while polling place wait times might affect voting behavior somewhat, the impact they have

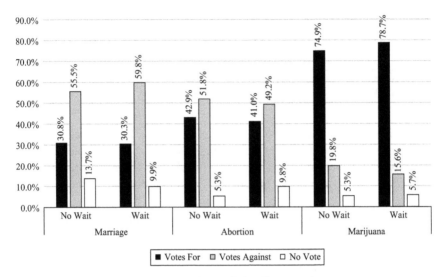

Figure 6.2   Vote Choice on More Easily Worded Ballot Questions.

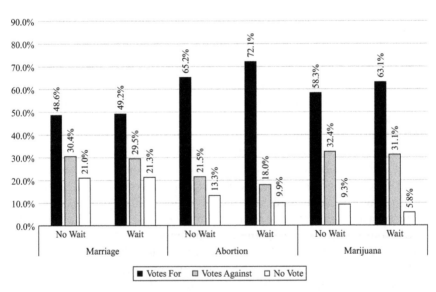

Figure 6.3   Vote Choice on More Difficultly Worded Ballot Questions.

may not be as strong as many have feared. There appear to be few differences in the voting tendencies of those subjects made to wait and those who were not delayed before voting. This finding comports with previous research suggesting that the value of voting can increase concomitantly with the amount of time and effort expended (i.e., Downs 1954).

Waiting and Vote Conformity (Hypothesis 3)

It is also possible that mock voters who waited may have completed their ballots but did so hastily and in a manner less reflective of their desired preferences. It is that question we next address. The mean voting conformity scores reported for each group on the "easy" ballot referenda in Table 6.2, however, suggest this may not be the case. Overall, those made to wait before voting exhibited similar conformity scores with those in the control group who had a wait-free voting experience. Across all three ballot measures, the control group maintained voting consistency about 67 percent of the time. In contrast, those who experienced a wait cast conforming votes about 71 percent of the time.

There was some variation across the issues, however. Respondents experiencing a wait time exhibited lower voting conformity than the control group on the same-sex marriage and abortion referenda, but counter to our expectation, those experiencing a wait voted in a more consistent manner than the control group on the marijuana referendum.[3] The group conformity scores, however, suggested that rather than the wait group being better able to vote in a manner consistent with their previously expressed positions on this issue, it is the control group's substantially lower consistency on this issue that accounts for the large intergroup difference. While both the control and the wait groups' level of conformity dropped substantially on the marijuana issue, the control group showed a larger decrease. While control-group subjects were able to cast conforming ballots about 80 percent of the time for the same-sex marriage and abortion referenda, they were able to do so in reference to legalizing marijuana only about 48 percent of the time. Similarly, the subjects made to wait were able to vote in a conforming manner only about 61 percent of the time when it came to legalizing marijuana but conformed about three-quarters of the time on the other ballot measures. It appears, then, that some ballot issues pose more of a problem for voters generally, but it

Table 6.2 Conformity Scores by Group—Easy Ballot Language

	Control Group	Wait	Difference	Significance
All Amendments	0.67 (148)	0.71 (76)	+0.04	0.384
Same-Sex Marriage Referendum	0.82 (246)	0.75 (120)	−0.07	0.234
Abortion Access Referendum	0.78 (246)	0.77 (120)	−0.01	0.832
Legalized Marijuana Referendum	0.48 (246)	0.61 (120)	+0.13	0.057

Notes: Cell entries are mean conformity scores for each group and valid number of cases (in parentheses). Significance levels are from two-tailed independent samples means tests.

may be the case that on such issues, waiting may actually help voters cope with the challenges presented by complex ballot initiatives.

Turning to the ballot measures with more difficult language, it appears that, overall, being asked to cast a ballot on ballot measures stated in more complex language was substantially more challenging to voters—across both treatments (see Table 6.3). In contrast to the high level (about 73 percent conformity) of consistent voting among all mock voters, regardless of group assignment, evident when dealing with the easier ballot language, only about 60 percent of the participants were able to cast ballots conforming to their previously stated preferences on the difficult-to-comprehend ballot questions.

Overall, those made to undertake a wait exhibited slightly lower conformity scores than those in the control group. Across all three "difficult" measures on the ballot, the control group maintained voting consistency about 62 percent of the time. In contrast, those made to wait voted in a manner consistent with their previously stated preferences about 58 percent of the time when faced with difficult ballot language.

Once again, the issue involved in the vote seemed to play a role as well, though the more difficultly worded same-sex marriage referendum, in addition to the marijuana issue, seemed to cause substantially less trouble for voters. Whether subjects were made to wait or not, their consistency on the abortion referendum with difficult language was well below that of other complicated referenda. As expected, though, both control and wait time group subjects showed a decrease in conformity on the abortion measure using language that was more complicated. These results further support our conclusion above that some particular issues pose more of a problem for voters generally, but, in some cases, waiting may actually be a benefit rather than a liability.

Wait Times, Stress, and Conformity

The results thus far suggest that experiencing a polling place wait is not consistently associated with lower voting conformity as we hypothesized.

Table 6.3 Conformity Scores by Group—Difficult Ballot Language

	Control Group	Wait	Difference	Significance
All Amendments	0.62 (124)	0.58 (61)	−0.04	0.388
Same-Sex Marriage Referendum	0.61 (246)	0.68 (118)	+0.07	0.377
Abortion Access Referendum	0.47 (245)	0.35 (120)	−0.12	0.114
Legalized Marijuana Referendum	0.78 (246)	0.82 (120)	+0.04	0.514

Notes: Cell entries are mean conformity scores for each group and valid number of cases (in parentheses). Significance levels are from two-tailed independent samples means tests.

Because we based our expectation on the assumption that stress placed on voters by polling place waits leads to impaired cognitive abilities, and consequently a nonconforming vote, we next tested the hypothetical linkages between wait time and stress, as well as stress and voting conformity.

As we did with regard to provisional ballots, we proposed a causal flow, shown in Figure 6.4, from a set of exogenous variables (wait time, non-citizen status, and political knowledge) through an intervening variable (stress, as measured previously) to an outcome variable (voting conformity). We again employed a multivariate path analysis, with the same expectations about the relationships between our variables, with the added expectation that those experiencing longer wait times would report high stress levels and lower voting conformity levels. We first predicted stress with wait time, political knowledge, and citizenship status. Then we predicted conformity with stress, wait time, and controls for citizenship status, political knowledge, political interest, partisan strength, ideological strength, voting history, perceived importance of voting, age, race, ethnicity, and sex.[4]

The results of our path analysis offer support for our contention that polling place wait times cause stress to voters.[5] At the same time, we saw only marginal support for our hypothesis that this added stress is associated with nonconforming ballots. As Figures 6.5 and 6.6 illustrate, longer wait times are associated with increased stress levels. Substantively, these results suggest that for each additional minute of waiting at the polling place, mock voters

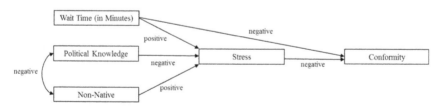

Figure 6.4　Hypothesized Relationships.

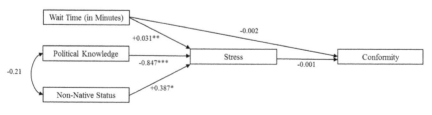

*p<0.10; **p<0.05; ***p<0.01

Figure 6.5　Wait Times, Stress, and Conformity—Easy Ballot Referenda.

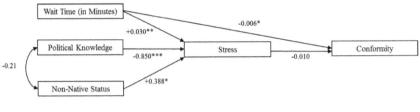

*p<0.10; **p<0.05; ***p<0.01

Figure 6.6   Wait Times, Stress, and Conformity—Difficult Ballot Referenda.

reported an increase of about 0.03, or about 0.5 percent on the full stress scale (and 0.7 percent on the truncated scale of observed values). Extrapolating from this estimate suggests that a typical mock voter made to wait for ten minutes would experience an increase of about 5 to 7 percent in his or her stress level.[6]

As expected, both those scoring lower on the political knowledge measure and non-native-American citizens exhibited more stress.[7] Also as expected, both stress and wait times showed negative, though mostly statistically insignificant, relationships with voting conformity. While wait time also showed a direct negative relationship with voting conformity, the coefficient was only statistically significant with regard to voting on the referenda issues presented with more complex wording. These results suggest there might be an interactive effect between waiting and ballot complexity.

Similar results emerged when examining the effects of wait times and stress on conformity for each issue separately. Turning first to the three ballot issues presented in simpler language, we saw that stress showed a negative relationship with voting conformity on same-sex marriage and abortion (see Figures 6.7a and 6.7b). Though one of the coefficients failed to meet traditional levels of statistical significance, these results provide some support for our hypothesis that increased polling place stress contributes to inconsistent voting. Counter to our expectation, however, subjects experiencing more stress appeared to be better able to cast a ballot that was consistent with their previously stated preference on this issue (see Figure 6.7c). This finding is somewhat surprising but does perhaps corroborate, as did our findings with regard to the effects ballot language had on voting on this issue, previous research showing improved decision-making capabilities through the use of cognitive heuristics (Payne, Bettman, and Johnson 1988).

The results for the direct effects of wait times on voting conformity offered us mixed support as well. While wait time showed a negative, but nonstatistically significant relationship to voting conformity for the same-sex marriage and abortion referenda, it was positively, and again nonsignificantly, related to conformity on the marijuana legalization referendum. Once again, we

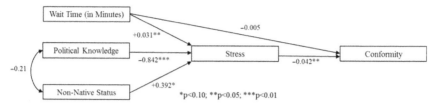

Figure 6.7a   Same-Sex Marriage Referendum (Easy Ballot Language).

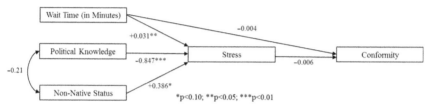

Figure 6.7b   Abortion Access Referendum (Easy Ballot Language).

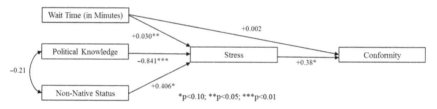

Figure 6.7c   Legalized Marijuana Referendum (Easy Ballot Language).

found our expectation that subjects experiencing longer wait times would be less likely to cast conforming ballots somewhat confirmed with regard to two amendments but contradicted with the third. The somewhat surprising finding that those made to wait reported more stress, but that this added anxiety was not associated with lower voting consistency, may be an effect of the simplicity of the ballot language for this issue. As reported in chapter 4, the more easily worded marijuana legalization amendment rates a 10.28 on the Flesch-Kinkaid scale. As currently enrolled college students, our subjects should have experienced little difficulty with a passage that is estimated to need about ten years of formal education to comprehend. And, as expected, our mock voters experiencing a wait did seem to have more trouble with the other two, more complexly worded, ballot measures.

The results for the more complex ballot language referenda showed a more consistent, though statistically nonsignificant, pattern (see Figures 6.8a–6.8c).[8] Across all three issues, stress exhibited a negative association

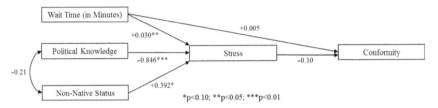

Figure 6.8a   Same-Sex Marriage Referendum (Difficult Ballot Language).

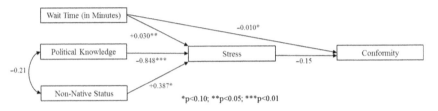

Figure 6.8b   Abortion Access Referendum (Difficult Ballot Language).

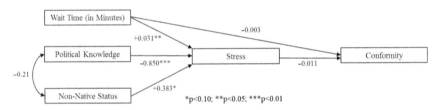

Figure 6.8c   Legalized Marijuana Referendum (Difficult Ballot Language).

with voting conformity. Though not meeting traditional levels of statistical significance, the negative coefficient suggests that those mock voters reporting more stress and facing difficult ballots were less likely to be able to cast votes that were consistent with their previously stated preferences. At the same time, the direct impact of wait times on voting conformity gained mixed support. While those asked to wait longer were less likely to cast ballots consistent with their earlier expressed preferences about abortion and marijuana legalization, they were more likely to conform on the same-sex marriage referendum (though only the abortion coefficient proved statistically significant).

These findings differ from those involving the more simply worded ballot measures, suggesting that there might be some interactive effects at play. While the mock voters made to wait were better able to vote in line with their preferences on the more comprehensible marijuana initiative, the same is not true when this policy was discussed in more complicated terms. Perhaps the cognitive shortcuts employed by our mock voters on the easier version of the measure were insufficient to overcome the added stress of the more difficult ballot wording on this issue.

Table 6.4 Direct and Indirect Effects of Wait Times on Voting Conformity

	Easy Language Amendments				Difficult Language Amendments			
	All Three	Same-Sex Marriage	Abortion Access	Legalized Marijuana	All Three	Same-Sex Marriage	Abortion Access	Legalized Marijuana
Direct effect	−0.002	−0.005	−0.004	+0.002	−0.006 [a]	+0.005	−0.010 [a]	−0.003
Indirect effect	−0.00003 [a]	−0.0013 [b]	−0.00019 [a]	+0.0011 [b]	−0.0003 [a]	−0.0003 [a]	−0.0045 [a]	−0.00034 [a]
Total effect	−0.00203	−0.0063	−0.0042	+0.0031	−0.0063	+0.0047	−0.0145	−0.00334

Notes: Direct effects estimated using the wait time-conformity coefficient. Indirect effects are estimated by taking the product of the wait time-stress and stress-conformity coefficients. Total effects are the sum of these two estimates.
[a] single coefficient in path model significant.
[b] both coefficients in path model statistically significant.

Notwithstanding statistical significance, the results suggest some potentially important substantive impacts. Table 6.4 presents the predicted direct and indirect effects of wait time. Looking at the more simply worded referenda issues, the combined negative effect that one minute of wait time directly exerted on voting conformity along with the indirect effect that a single minute of waiting exerted by increasing stress levels, which in turn influenced conformity, ranged from about −0.2 percent for overall conformity on all three referenda to about −0.6 percent on the same-sex marriage issue. Extrapolating, this suggests that a ten-minute wait would decrease voting conformity on the same-sex marriage referendum by about 6 percent and on the abortion issue by about 4 percent. Conversely, the same ten-minute wait improved conformity by about 3 percent when it came to voting on legalizing marijuana.

The combined negative effects that a ten minute wait has on the more complexly worded referenda were more pronounced, ranging between about −3 percent (marijuana ballot measure) and −15 percent (abortion referendum). Again, however, there was some variation across issues, with a similar wait leading to only an estimated 5 percent increase in conformity on the same-sex marriage question.

DISCUSSION

Taken together, these results suggest that polling place wait times have little, if any, direct impact on the ability of voters to cast ballots in a way that is consistent with their previously stated beliefs. While voters experiencing a longer wait did appear to be about 1 percent less likely to vote their previously stated preference on a difficultly worded abortion issue, waiting exerted no direct effect on voting conformity for any of the other referenda. We did find, however, consistent support for our contention that longer wait times are associated with an increase in the stress felt by voters. And with regard to some issues, this increased stress affected voters' ability to cast their ballots in a way consistent with their previously reported beliefs. Voters who faced more simply worded same-sex marriage referendum measures and who were made to wait appeared to vote in a conforming manner somewhat less than other voters. For those voters, a ten-minute wait was predicted to decrease their ability to vote in a conforming manner by about 1.3 percent. At the same time, our models suggest that the same wait will lead voters to cast conforming ballots about 1.1 percent more often when facing a simply worded referendum on legalizing marijuana.[9] Therefore, while waiting may exert, directly or indirectly, some effects on voting conformity, the impact is, at most, mixed and varied across ballot issues. These results speak to concerns about some of the polling place glitches brought to light in recent elections, suggesting that the much reported deleterious effects of long wait times may indeed affect overall voter turnout but may not be much of a problem for most voters who have the wherewithal to withstand the delay.

These findings comport with those regarding the minimal effects that the turnout literature reports regarding waiting. Further, previous research suggests that waiting-induced stress can be attenuated when a wait is expected and does not exceed the expected duration (Leclerc, Schmitt, and Dube 1995). Just as voters in recent elections have become aware that they are likely to face long polling place wait times, the students who served as our mock voters were also accustomed to being asked to wait for unexplained, indefinite amounts of time at various academic offices across campus.

Moving beyond polling place wait times, the full multivariate analyses again showed that some segments of our mock electorate experienced more stress and exhibited less voting conformity than others. The more knowledgeable, as well as those who viewed voting as more important and had more voting experience, reported less anxiety and were better able to vote in a way that conformed with their previously stated opinions. Minority participants, as well as those who were not born in the United States, again exhibited lower levels of voting conformity.

These findings further highlight the potential difficulties different segments of the electorate might face at the polling place. Given the difficulties some members of the electorate have at the polling place, it is possible that being made to wait may impact some potential voters more than others. We address this question in the next chapter by investigating the ways in which polling place wait times, as well as provisional ballots, affected those members of our mock electorate who already found the act of voting more stressful and/ or had difficulty casting ballots in a manner that reflected their preferences. In addition, we also build on findings from chapter 4 regarding the ways in which administrator characteristics might serve to enhance the impact of other barriers voters encounter at the polling place.

NOTES

1. Independent samples comparison of means tests show no statistically significant differences in non-voting rates between the waiting and non-waiting groups on the more simply worded marriage and marijuana ballot measures, and a marginally significant (p=0.10) difference for the abortion item.

2. Independent samples comparison of means tests show no statistically significant differences in support rates between the waiting and non-waiting groups on the more simply worded ballot measures.

3. It is also interesting to note that the difference in conformity scores is only statistically significant for the marijuana referendum, as well.

4. The deletion of insignificant control variables in the vote conformity models significantly reduces the fit between the model and the data. Consequently, the fuller models are presented here.

5. Full regression results available from authors upon request.

6. Predicted effect calculated using unstandardized regression coefficients from the full path analysis regressions.

7. Non-citizens also show generally lower levels of voting conformity.

8. Non-citizens, however, show more consistency, again exhibiting more stress and generally lower levels of voting conformity.

9. These results echo the modest findings reported by Highton (2006) regarding the impact of voting machine available on turnout.

Chapter 7

Are the Barriers Higher for Some Voters?

The Conditional Effects of Polling Place Stressors

"We're talking about huge chunks of the electorate that are in danger of being disenfranchised," said Jonathan Stein, a staff attorney with Asian Americans Advancing Justice-California (*Los Angeles Times* 2017). Concerns such as the one expressed above highlight the distinctive ways that voting barriers might impact certain segments of the voting public more than others. The potential representational impact of voting barriers has attracted the attention of a number of scholars over the years, with some arguing that contextual factors such as union strength, party ideology, organizational capacity, and competitiveness can lead to turnout differences that could have potential policy implications (Leighley and Nagler 2007; Hill and Leighley 1993, 1996). Other studies, however, show that differential patterns of turnout do not explain representational interests related to social class as much as the electorate's demographic characteristics (Hill and Leighley 1994; Leighley and Nagler 1992). Together these studies highlight the importance of recognizing both the electoral context and the disparate impact that context might have on different segments of the electorate.

While many voters may find complicated ballot language troublesome, such language might serve to drive only some voters away from the voting booth altogether. Similarly, being made to vote a provisional ballot or wait an undetermined amount of time before casting a ballot might stress some potential voters more than others. Put quite simply, voting barriers do not affect all voters equally. For example, regulatory barriers, even when removed, do not influence noninterested voters (Bowler and Donovan 2008). In other words, voters who are not interested in the election cycle are not going to become interested and participate just because it is easier to participate. Likewise, early voting merely conveniences those who would have voted anyway

(Neeley and Richardson 2001), so new voters are not motivated to participate just because they can do so at their leisure.

There are particular portions of the electorate that are more likely to be exposed to certain barriers. For example, transient and minority voters are more likely to use provisional ballots than other voters (Alvarez and Hall 2009). Furthermore, precincts with higher proportions of younger residents show a higher rate of provisional balloting (Alvarez and Hall 2009). Additionally, districts with low socioeconomic status are more likely to have fewer polling booths and machines, which leads to longer lines. Thus, we expected certain socioeconomic factors to influence voting obstacles' effects on voters. In fact, our experimental participants represented a racially diverse, young (college-aged) group, which is precisely the demographic group that we might expect to change households frequently (Bleemer et al. 2014). In addition, we expected race and age to show a stronger relationship to both roll-off and voting conformity among the group who either voted provisionally or waited in line for a lengthy period of time (hypotheses 5.1a and 1b).

As the literature demonstrates (Cobb and Hedges 2004; Alvarez and Hall 2006; Kimball and Foley 2009), many of the decisions about provisional ballot use are left to undertrained poll workers; these workers' interactions with voters often lower both voter efficacy and trust in the voting process (Hall, Monson, and Patterson 2009). Additionally, the length of time it can take to vote can depend on the administrator's knowledge and expediency. Administrators may take longer to address some voters' needs, thus lengthening other voters' waiting times. In this chapter, we investigate the ways in which administrator and voter characteristics might interact with provisional ballot use and polling place wait times.

THE IMPORTANCE OF ELECTION
ADMINISTRATOR CHARACTERISTICS

We first investigated the ways in which administrator characteristics might serve to either alleviate or intensify the effects of polling place barriers in our examination of ballot language complexity (see chapter 4). Our earlier investigation revealed only limited effects for administrator characteristics. Based on those results, we might not expect to find many administrator effects here, either. At the same time, there is good reason to believe that provisional ballot use and polling place wait times are more sensitive to the ways in which voters interact with election administrators. Since poll workers do not directly control ballot language, voters may not be associating them with the challenges that complex ballot language present, but the same is not the case for provisional ballots and polling place waiting. Poll workers represent the point of contact between voters and these barriers; after all, an election administrator is the official who must inform voters that they must vote provisionally and is the person who must ask voters to wait, providing any (or no) explanation as to why and for how long. Consequently, we next explore the possibility that poll worker characteristics might play a more important role in exacerbating the effects of provisional ballot use and polling place waiting than they did in enhancing the effects of ballot complexity

Minority Administrators and Racial Homogeneity

State laws dealing with voter registration have historically been contentious, especially concerning the way these statutes impact minorities and members of lower socioeconomic classes. America's history of discrimination and blatant racism at polling and registration centers has created an environment of mistrust among large segments of the electorate. This sentiment most obviously pervades black communities, where trust in the registration process and in vote efficacy is minimal (Parent and Shrum 1985). Furthermore, voting inspires an inherent desire for privacy in many citizens, especially those who feel least self-confident about their political prowess (Gerber et al. 2013). Thus, certain members of the electorate are likely to be especially irritated by any perceived challenges or impediments to their voting rights. The precarious government-voter dynamic that arises from this sort of distrust often inhibits turnout and can be a detriment to the political process as a whole. Any additional stressors involved in the registration-voting process, such as a requirement to vote provisionally or the need to endure a wait before voting, could be enough to alter vote choice, encourage roll-off, or deter participation altogether. Taken together, these conditions lead us to believe that subjects who were either made to vote a provisional ballot or were forced to wait before voting by an election administrator who is a member of a minority race might have experienced even higher levels of stress and have exhibited lower levels of voting conformity (hypothesis 5.2a). At the same time, however, it is important to remember that minority voters may be comforted by the presence of a minority poll worker.

Administrator Sex

Similarly, we investigated potential gender effects by testing to see if the effects of provisional ballot use and polling place wait times were heightened when mock voters were confronted with a female administrator. Research shows that women who administer polling interviews tend to get more negative reports from respondents than their male peers do (Groves and Fultz 1985). Interaction with a female interviewer can affect behavior, as well; poll respondents have been shown to express more egalitarian attitudes and to be more supportive of female issues when the interviewer was female (Kane and Macaulay 1993; Leuptow, Moser, and Pendleton 1990). While our participants were not responding to the administrator directly, we expected the same negative reaction to female poll workers that Groves and Fultz (1985) found. Similarly, as seen in interview research (Kane and Macaulay 1993; Leuptow, Moser, and Pendleton 1990), reactions to female election workers might lead to inconsistent voting. Consequently, we expected those voters who were compelled by a female administrator to either vote provisionally or wait before casting a vote to report higher levels of stress, and consequently lower voting consistency, than those who encountered a male administrator (hypothesis 5.2c).

Administrator Demeanor

Expanding on the ways in which similarity between voter and administrator might condition the impact of provisional ballots and wait times, we investigated the ways in which shared regional identification between voters and administrators might mitigate the stress associated with these obstacles. Taken together, these conditions might have made our mock provisional voters more comfortable with the process and less reactionary to voting rights challenges when they were challenged by a Southern mock election official. Thus, we expected mock provisional voters who encountered a Southern administrator to report lower levels of stress, and consequently less ballot roll-off and higher voting consistency, than those who faced a non-Southern administrator (hypothesis 5.2d).

THE IMPORTANCE OF VOTER COMMITMENT

While poll workers play a vital role in the voters' ability to vote and to vote consistently, it is important to remember that some voters are likely to be more motivated to punch through polling place barriers than others. Experienced voters and those who feel that voting is important may be more readily equipped to overcome obstacles they might encounter at the polling place. Frequent voters who are familiar with the electoral process have previously experienced the various Election Day activities and are more likely to understand both the requirements (e.g., photo identification, prior registration) and the potential complications that voting entails. Similarly, people who feel that voting is important, even if they do not have a long voting history, are likely to have paid particular attention to relevant voting requirements. Thus, we expected that provisional ballot subjects who reported frequently voting in the past (hypothesis 6.1) and those who felt that voting was more important (hypothesis 6.2) to report lower stress levels, and consequently higher voting consistency, than those who reported not voting as frequently in the past or who felt that voting was not as important.

Investigating the Conditional Effects of Provisional Ballots and Polling Place Wait Times

To test the possible modulating effects of election administrator character-istics and voter commitment, we first examined our mock voters' reported stress levels as they encountered the combination of polling place barriers and poll workers of different types. We then turned to the question of whether the voters' commitment to electoral participation reduced their stress levels and boosted their ability to vote in a way that conformed to their previously expressed preferences. As in previous chapters, we reported bivariate correla-tion and means tests comparison results. We compared the mean stress and mean conformity levels of our subjects who faced either a polling place wait or a provisional ballot in combination with election administrators of differ-ent types. Similarly, we compared the levels of reported stress levels of mock voters of different commitment levels and their ability to vote in a conform-ing manner with similar statistical tests.

Conditional Effects of Provisional Ballots

Thus far, our expectations about provisional ballots' impact on voting behav-ior have garnered little support. It is still possible, however, that provisional ballots might affect some voters more than others. To investigate the pos-sibility that provisional ballots might prove more challenging to voters with lower socioeconomic status, we investigated the ways in which provisional ballots affected younger and minority mock voters, in particular (hypotheses 5.1a and b).[1] We first compared the correlation between age and both reported stress levels and voting conformity for provisional and non-provisional voters. The bivariate coefficients shown in Table 7.1, like those we have reported previously, range from −1 to +1, with values closer to 0 indicating weaker relationships and those closer to either +1 or −1 indicating stronger relationships. Negative values can be interpreted to mean that older voters reported lower stress or exhibited lower levels of voting conformity (and, conversely, that younger voters reported higher stress and higher levels of voting conformity).

The coefficients revealed an inconsistent pattern. While older voters, regardless of the type of ballot used, tended to report lower overall stress lev-els, the relationship between age and voting conformity varied by provisional

Table 7.1 Provisional Ballots and Voter Age

	Stress	Easy Ballot Wording			Difficult Ballot Wording		
		Marriage	Abortion	Marijuana	Marriage	Abortion	Marijuana
Non-Provisional Voters	−0.085 (229)	−0.105 (193)	−0.052 (205)	0.003 (210)	−0.205** (172)	−0.001 (196)	0.109 (206)
Provisional Voters	−0.098 (108)	−0.109 (97)	0.040 (103)	0.048 (104)	0.200 (85)	−0.066 (88)	−0.092 (105)

Notes: Cell entries are Pearson's r bivariate correlations and number of valid cases (in parentheses). ***$p<0.01$ (two-tailed).

status. Taking the more easily worded questions first, we see that older voters, provisional and non-provisional alike, tended to exhibit lower voting conformity on the same-sex marriage and legalized marijuana referenda. Voting on the abortion question, however, showed varied effects across ballot types. Older non-provisional voters showed less voting conformity than their junior counterparts, but more senior provisional voters were better able to cast votes that conformed to their previously stated positions than were younger voters. A similar divergence appears with regard to the more difficultly worded same-sex amendment, and the opposite effect occurs on the legalized marijuana ballot issue. Taken together, these mixed results suggest that provisional ballots may not be consistently causing younger voters more trouble than their elders.

Some have claimed that provisional ballots represent a particular challenge to the nonwhite sector of the electorate since minority voters more frequently find their voting rights challenged (Fitrakis 2014). To investigate possible conditioning effects of voter race (hypothesis 5.11), we compared the mean reported stress and observed voting conformity levels of provisional and non-provisional mock voters by race (see Table 7.2). Though the difference of means does not rise to traditional levels of statistical significance for minority voters, both provisional and non-provisional minority voters reported higher stress levels than nonminority voters. Importantly, and contrary to our hypothesis, minority provisional voters reported lower levels of stress than minority non-provisional voters. Similar results emerged from our examination of voting conformity levels. Minority voters made to cast a provisional ballot were better able to cast a vote consistent with their previously stated preferences than were minority voters allowed to cast a non-provisional ballot. The same was true for nonminority voters on all but one ballot proposal. Provisional balloters exhibited a very slight tendency to vote inconsistently on the more complexly worded same-sex marriage amendment, although the difference was miniscule.

Taken together, these results suggest that provisional ballots may not be a problem for voters, including those whom we might most expect to have difficulty with them. But the voter does not operate in isolation on Election Day. Upon arrival at the polling place, would-be voters interact with an election administrator, and it is possible that polling place worker characteristics might play a role in provisional ballots' impact on voters. To investigate our hypotheses that election administrators' race, sex, and demeanor might accentuate the stressful effects of using provisional ballots, we examined provisional and non-provisional voters' mean reported stress levels and observed the subjects' voting conformity across a variety of election administrator types.

Table 7.2　Provisional Ballots and Voter Race

	Stress	Easy Ballot Wording			Difficult Ballot Wording		
		Marriage	Abortion	Marijuana	Marriage	Abortion	Marijuana
Non-Provisional							
Minority	1.47 (123)	0.77 (103)	0.74 (116)	0.50 (117)	0.63 (87)	0.37 (106)	0.78 (114)
Nonminority	1.24 (123)	0.81 (90)	0.81 (90)	0.51 (94)	0.66 (85)	0.04 (91)	0.82 (93)
Provisional							
Minority	0.84 (58)	0.84 (50)	0.89 (50)	0.70 (56)	0.72 (46)	0.49 (45)	0.90 (59)
Nonminority	0.60 (50)	0.87 (47)	0.84 (53)	0.56 (58)	0.63 (39)	0.36 (43)	0.85 (46)

Notes: Cell entries are mean conformity scores for each group and number of valid cases (in parentheses).

Table 7.3 Provisional Ballots and Election Administrator Characteristics

	Stress	Easy Ballot Wording			Difficult Ballot Wording		
		Marriage	Abortion	Marijuana	Marriage	Abortion	Marijuana
Hypothesis 5.2a							
Non-Provisional Voters							
Minority Administrator	1.28 (64)	0.83 (53)	0.78 (58)	0.58 (59)	0.59 (46)	0.38 (55)	0.86 (58)
Nonminority Administrator	1.39 (165)	0.77 (140)	0.77 (148)	0.53 (152)	0.67 (126)	0.42 (142)	0.77 (149)
Provisional Voters							
Minority Administrator	0.91 (35)	0.94 (32)	0.77 (35)	0.56 (34)	0.67 (30)	0.35 (34)	0.86 (35)
Non-minority Administrator	0.64 (73)	0.82 (65)	0.91 (68)	0.67 (70)	0.67 (55)	0.46 (54)	0.91 (70)
Hypothesis 5.2b							
Non-Provisional Voters							
Same Race Administrator	1.24 (103)	0.78 (82)	0.82 (96)	0.59 (96)	0.60 (71)	0.36 (89)	0.85 (94)
Different Race Administrator	1.50 (126)	0.79 (111)	0.72 (110)	0.48 (115)	0.70 (101)	0.47 (108)	0.73 (113)
Provisional Voters							
Same Race Administrator	0.84 (57)	0.88 (48)	0.85 (49)	0.63 (50)	0.74 (42)	0.40 (45)	0.85 (52)
Different Race Administrator	0.63 (51)	0.83 (49)	0.88 (54)	0.64 (43)	0.60 (43)	0.44 (43)	0.90 (53)
Hypothesis 5.2c							
Non-Provisional Voters							
Male Administrator	1.49 (79)	0.76 (62)	0.79 (71)	0.51 (71)	0.62 (58)	0.45 (65)	0.80 (71)
Female Administrator	1.29 (150)	0.80 (131)	0.75 (135)	0.56 (140)	0.66 (114)	0.39 (132)	0.79 (136)
Provisional Voters							
Male Administrator	0.67 (38)	0.83 (35)	0.89 (35)	0.84 (37)	0.63 (30)	0.44 (32)	0.93 (40)
Female Administrator	0.76 (70)	0.87 (62)	0.85 (68)	0.52 (67)	0.69 (55)	0.41 (56)	0.85 (65)
Hypothesis 5.2d							

(*Continued*)

Table 7.3 Provisional Ballots and Election Administrator Characteristics (*Continued*)

	Stress	Easy Ballot Wording			Difficult Ballot Wording		
		Marriage	Abortion	Marijuana	Marriage	Abortion	Marijuana
Non-Provisional Voters							
Southern Administrator	1.63 (67)	0.78 (59)	0.77 (61)	0.60 (62)	0.69 (52)	0.42 (55)	0.80 (61)
Non-Southern Administrator	1.25 (162)	0.79 (134)	0.77 (145)	0.52 (149)	0.63 (120)	0.41 (142)	0.79 (146)
Provisional Voters							
Southern Administrator	0.70 (28)	0.84 (25)	0.92 (25)	0.93 (27)	0.64 (22)	0.50 (22)	0.93 (28)
Non-Southern Administrator	0.74 (80)	0.86 (72)	0.85 (78)	0.53 (77)	0.68 (63)	0.39 (66)	0.86 (77)

Notes: Cell entries are the mean stress level reported on the 16-point stress scale, mean voting conformity levels, and number of valid cases (in parentheses).

We first tested to see if mock provisional voters who were confronted by a minority mock election administration reported higher levels of stress (hypothesis 2a), and consequently more ballot roll-off and lower voting consistency. We then examined potential gender effects, by testing to see if the effects of provisional ballot use were heightened when a mock voter was confronted with a female administrator (hypothesis 3). Similarly, we investigated those who faced a non-Southern administrator (hypothesis 4).

Examining the top section of Table 7.3, we see that our provisional mock voters who faced a minority administrator reported higher levels of stress than when they faced a nonminority administrator. Though not reaching statistical significance, this difference does suggest that the combination of minority polling place workers and provisional ballot use might be putting voters under additional stress. Interestingly, the same is not true for our non-provisional voters, who reported feeling less stress when facing a minority mock election administrator. Once again, however, it appears that our provisional mock voters were able to cope with any additional stresses and, on almost all of the ballot measures, voted more consistently with their preferences when using a provisional ballot. Only on the more easily worded same-sex amendment did provisional voters who faced a minority poll worker show less voting consistency, and this effect held across ballot wording difficulty level.

To investigate whether such effects might extend to voters facing an election administrator with whom they share a racial identity (hypothesis 5.2b), we repeated our analysis, comparing provisional and non-provisional voters who faced congruent and incongruent racial polling place exchanges. Contrary to expectation, provisional voters facing an election administrator of the same race reported higher levels of overall stress, while non-provisional voters reacted as we expected, reporting more stress when facing a poll worker of a different race. Also contrary to our expectations, provisional voters facing incongruent racial interactions consistently showed higher levels of voting conformity on the legalized marijuana measure. Overall, when taken along with our previous findings with regard to election administrator characteristics, these findings offer little support for arguments that poll workers' race and sex exacerbate potential provisional ballot use problems.

We saw similar results when we investigated the effects of election administrator gender (hypothesis 5.2c). Provisional mock voters reported higher stress levels when they faced a female poll worker, but the non-provisional voters reported the opposite. In contrast to the findings regarding administrator race, there was more consistent evidence that this added stress might be causing provisional voters problems in the voting booth. On both the abortion access and legalized marijuana ballot measures, provisional voters were less able to cast conforming votes when they faced a female poll worker. In contrast, it is important to recognize that non-provisional voters showed a tendency to vote equally or more consistently when facing a female election administrator on four of the referenda, as well. Overall, then, any effects that election administrator gender exerts are likely to be quite limited.

Perhaps descriptive characteristics like sex and race have less to do with stressing voters than does the treatment voters receive from poll workers. While we did not explicitly vary the rudeness with which we interacted with our subjects, our mock election administrators came from varied backgrounds, including two with Southern upbringing. To investigate the possibility that our mock voters (largely Southerners themselves) had a better rapport with the Southern administrators, which might have lowered the voters' stress levels, we repeated our mean stress and conformity levels comparison for provisional and non-provisional voters facing administrators with different demeanors (hypothesis 5.2d). Provisional and non-provisional voters again diverged in their reactions to the administrator; mock provisional voters reported slightly higher overall stress levels and exhibited voting conformity levels between 7 percent and 40 percent lower on the abortion access and legalized marijuana ballot referenda. At the same time, non-provisional voters who interacted with a Southern administrator reported lower stress levels and much smaller and more inconsistent changes in voting conformity. Although these results are limited, they suggest that provisional ballot use might be less troublesome when voters experience friendlier and less confrontational interchanges with poll workers.

As one last test of the conditioning effect that voter commitment might have on provisional ballot use, we examined the ways in which both a familiarity with voting and a strong desire to cast a ballot might alleviate the effects that provisional ballots have on voter stress and voting behavior (hypotheses 6.1 and 6.2). We return to our use of correlation coefficients ranging from −1 to +1 in Table 7.4, correlating the frequency with which each subject reported voting in past elections on a six-point scale (ranging from "never" to "every election") and how important each subject felt voting was on a four-point scale (from "not at all important" to "very important") with reported stress and observed voting conformity. The initial results regarding voting experience supported our hypothesis. Among both non-provisional and provisional voters, subjects who reported voting more frequently in past elections reported lower overall stress at our mock polling place. Importantly, the effect was stronger among non-provisional voters, suggesting that, even though past polling place experience helps to mitigate stress, being forced to vote provisionally still places voters under more strain. A similar pattern developed with regard to voting behavior; while non-provisional voters with more experience at the polls were more likely to conform on four of the six ballot measures, provisional voters who reported a more frequent voting history were only able to vote more consistently on the more difficulty worded

Table 7.4 Frequency, Importance, and the Provisional Ballots

	Stress	Easy Ballot Wording			Difficult Ballot Wording		
		Marriage	Abortion	Marijuana	Marriage	Abortion	Marijuana
Non-Provisional Voters							
Frequent Voter	-0.050 (229)	0.020 (193)	-0.020 (206)	0.030 (211)	-0.208*** (172)	0.100 (197)	0.090 (207)
Voting Important	-0.140** (229)	0.054 (193)	0.076 (206)	-0.091 (211)	0.045 (172)	0.019 (197)	0.034 (122)
Provisional Voters							
Frequent Voter	-0.002 (108)	-0.033 (97)	-0.187 (104)	-0.007 (85)	0.105 (88)	-0.041 (105)	-0.008 (63)
Voting Important	0.054 (108)	-0.118 (97)	-0.02 (103)	-0.013 (104)	0.081 (85)	0.024 (88)	0.063 (105)

Notes: Cell entries are bivariate correlation coefficients and number of valid cases (in parentheses). **p<0.05 (two-tailed), ***p<0.01.

same-sex marriage amendment. So, while an understanding of Election Day procedures might lessen provisional voters' anxiety, it might not be enough to ensure they cast ballots in the intended manner.

Casting an eye, finally, to the impact that a strong desire to cast a ballot might have, we saw differing results for provisional and non-provisional voters. While, as expected, non-provisional voters who rated voting importance higher reported less stress, provisional voters reported the opposite. Voters who viewed voting as more important and had their rights challenged expressed higher levels of angst, and this heightened stress might be part of the reason why, on the simply worded ballot questions, these voters were less likely to be able to cast a vote that was consistent with their previously stated preferences. Conversely, non-provisional voters who stressed voting importance were better able to cast conforming votes on five of the six amendments with which they were presented. So, while voters' feelings about vote sanctity may be a motivating factor, those feelings may also cause those who have their voting rights challenged to experience anguish, which could lead to mistakes in the voting booth.

The Conditional Effects of Polling Place Waiting

So far, our results (presented in chapter 6) offer only marginal support for our expectations about the impact that polling place wait times have on voting behavior. It is still possible, however, that waiting might affect some voters more than others. Consequently, we investigated the possibility that polling place wait times might impact voters with lower socioeconomic status more than other voters by investigating the ways in which waiting affected younger and minority mock voters in particular (hypotheses 5.1a and b). We first compared the correlation between age and both reported stress levels and voting conformity for waiting and non-waiting voters. The bivariate coefficients are shown in Table 7.5. As a reminder, these values range from −1 to +1, with values closer to 0 indicating weaker relationships and those closer to either +1 or −1 indicating stronger relationships. Negative values can be interpreted to mean that older voters reported lower stress or exhibited lower voting conformity levels (and, conversely, that younger voters reported higher stress and higher voting conformity levels).

The results first suggest that older voters, whether they were asked to wait or not, expressed less stress about the voting process. Importantly, however, the relationship between age and polling place stress was much stronger for our mock voters who experienced a wait; that is, younger voters who were made to wait were much more likely to report feeling anxiety than their older counterparts. The same negative relationship emerges when examining the relationship between age and voting conformity on the more easily

Table 7.5 Polling Place Waiting and Voter Age

	Stress	Easy Ballot Wording			Difficult Ballot Wording		
		Marriage	*Abortion*	*Marijuana*	*Marriage*	*Abortion*	*Marijuana*
Non-Waiting Voters	−0.003 (223)	0.050 (245)	0.071 (245)	−0.007 (245)	−0.120 (245)	0.095 (244)	−0.042 (245)
Waiting Voters	−0.191** (113)	−0.102 (120)	−0.016 (120)	−0.027 (120)	0.071 (118)	0.008 (120)	0.043 (120)

Notes: Cell entries are Pearson's r bivariate correlation coefficients and valid number of cases (in parentheses). **$p<0.05$.

comprehended ballot measures. Younger mock voters exhibited lower voting conformity on all three amendments. In contrast, younger non-waiting subjects showed this tendency for only the easily worded legalized marijuana referendum. A different picture appears in the results for the more difficultly worded ballot measures. In all three issue domains, young, waiting voters showed higher voting conformity, while non-waiting younger voters voted more consistently than their older counterparts on only the difficult abortion access ballot item. Taken together, these mixed results imply that polling place wait times might not be consistently causing younger voters more trouble than their elders.

Some have claimed that polling place wait times represent a particular challenge to the nonwhite sector of the electorate, since minority voters more frequently find themselves in precincts with a shortage of working voting machines (Kropf and Kimball 2013). To investigate possible conditioning effects of voter race, we compared the mean reported stress and observed voting conformity levels of waiting and non-waiting mock voters by race (see Table 7.6.). As these results indicate, minority voters, waiting and non-waiting alike, reported higher stress levels than nonminority voters. Importantly, though, the difference in stress reported by nonminority mock voters made to wait and those not made to wait was larger than the difference between that of minority voters. The mean stress level reported by waiting minority voters was less than one-half of one point higher than that of their non-waiting counterparts, while the anxiety expressed by nonminority waiters was about three-quarters of a point higher. While not overwhelming, this difference is still impressive given the limited stress range reported by our subjects. The voting conformity levels results are more mixed; on only half of the measures did waiting minority mock voters appear substantively less likely to conform. Minority subjects who were asked to wait showed voting consistency levels between three and 14 percent lower when first asked to wait. At the same time, nonminority mock voters who were subjected to a wait were able to vote equally or more consistently on four of the six of the referenda.

Altogether, these results suggest that polling place wait times may not consistently be a problem for voters, but they do seem to cause more trouble for minority voters. And, importantly, the polling place involves not only the voter but also election officials. It is possible that polling place worker characteristics might either calm or exacerbate the irksome effects of waiting. We investigated our hypotheses that the race, sex, or demeanor of election administrators might accentuate the stressful effects of polling place wait times (hypotheses 5.2a, b, c, and d), with an examination of the

Table 7.6 Polling Place Waiting and Voter Race/Ethnicity

	Stress	Easy Ballot Wording			Difficult Ballot Wording		
		Marriage	*Abortion*	*Marijuana*	*Marriage*	*Abortion*	*Marijuana*
No Wait							
Nonminority	0.80**	0.87	0.84	0.54	0.67	0.48	0.82
Minority	1.15**	0.81	0.81	0.57	0.62	0.42	0.84
Wait							
Nonminority	1.46	0.76	0.84	0.64	0.69	0.28	0.85
Minority	1.52	0.75	0.70	0.58	0.67	0.42	0.79

Notes: Cell entries are the mean stress level reported on the 16-point stress scale and mean voting conformity levels. Cell entries in bold are statistically significant at **p<0.05 (two-tailed).

Table 7.7 Polling Place Waiting and Election Administrator Characteristics

	Stress	Easy Ballot Wording			Difficult Ballot Wording		
		Marriage	Abortion	Marijuana	Marriage	Abortion	Marijuana
Hypothesis 5.2a							
No Wait							
Nonminority Administrator	0.99	0.81	0.85	0.57	0.67	0.49	0.81
Minority Administrator	0.99	0.89	0.77	0.52	0.60	0.37	0.86
Wait							
Nonminority Administrator	1.45	0.74	0.76	0.58	0.67	0.35	0.78
Minority Administrator	1.62	0.79	0.80	0.73	0.71	0.39	0.95
Hypothesis 5.2b							
No Wait							
Same Race Administrator	1.01	0.86	0.81	0.57	0.62	0.42	0.84
Different Race Administrator	0.97	0.82	0.83	0.53	0.66	0.48	0.81
Wait							
Same Race Administrator	1.35	0.73	0.86**	0.67	0.69	0.28	0.86
Different Race Administrator	1.67	0.79	0.66**	0.53	0.67	0.43	0.76
Hypothesis 5.2c							
No Wait							
Male Administrator	1.03	0.83	0.81	0.63	0.59	0.46	0.85
Female Administrator	0.97	0.85	0.83	0.51	0.67	0.44	0.81
Wait							
Male Administrator	1.62	0.71	0.76	0.61	0.69	0.41	0.83
Female Administrator	1.42	0.78	0.77	0.61	0.67	0.33	0.81
Hypothesis 5.2d							
No Wait							
Non-Southern Administrator	0.92	0.84	0.81	0.50**	0.63	0.42	0.82
Southern Administrator	1.18	0.84	0.85	0.70**	0.67	0.52	0.85
Wait							
Non-Southern Administrator	1.42	0.76	0.77	0.57	0.68	0.37	0.81
Southern Administrator	1.62	0.74	0.76	0.70	0.68	0.32	0.82

Notes: Cell entries are the mean stress level reported on the 16-point stress scale and mean voting conformity levels. **$p<0.05$ (two-tailed) on independent sample comparison of means tests.

mean reported stress levels and observed voting conformity of waiting and non-waiting voters across a variety of election administrator types.

The results shown at the top of Table 7.7 largely contradict our expectation about administrator effects on stress but show some support for our assertion about their effect on voting behavior. While non-waiting voters expressed the same level of stress, regardless of the race of the election administrator, those who withstood a wait reported more stress when asked to do so by a minority administrator. Despite expressing more anxiety when interacting with a minority poll worker, those made to wait exhibited higher levels of voting conformity on all of the ballot measures. And, interestingly, ballot wording difficulty seemed to make little difference. The conformity level difference between subjects who were asked to wait by a minority mock poll worker and those who were asked to do so by a nonminority mock election official was about the same whether voters were weighing in on an easily understood or a more difficult to understand amendment proposal. And the non-waiting mock voters generally exhibited the opposite behavior; on four of the six ballot measures, non-waiting subjects who faced a minority election administrator showed an impaired ability to cast a consistent ballot.

To see if a shared identity between voter and poll worker might help alleviate polling place anxieties and its effects, we repeated our analysis comparing waiting and non-waiting voters facing congruent and incongruent racial polling place exchanges (hypothesis 5.2b). Waiting and non-waiting subjects diverged in their response to voter–poll worker racial similarity. While non-waiting participants reported higher levels of stress when dealing with a mock election administrator of their own race, those who were asked to wait appeared less stressed when asked to do so by someone with whom they shared a racial identity. This lessened anxiety comports with higher voting consistency among this group on four of the six ballot proposals; whether navigating difficult to understand ballot language or not, mock voters who were asked to wait by a mock election administrator of the same race were better able to cast a vote consistent with their previously stated positions two out of three times. Along with our previous findings with regard to election administrator characteristics, these findings offer some support for the argument that poll workers' race exacerbate potential problems caused by polling place wait times.

Our data offer less support when investigating the effects of election administrator gender (hypothesis 5.2c). Mock voters who faced a female polling place worker reported lower overall stress levels, whether they were made to wait or not. However, there does appear to be something of an effect on voting conformity. Those participants who were asked to wait before voting and encountered a female mock election administrator showed the same or a better ability to vote consistently on the more easily worded proposals than those voters who were asked to wait and interacted with a male poll worker. In contrast, voting conformity on all three of the more complex referenda was lower among those who were asked to wait by a female mock election administrator.

Moving from more descriptive characteristics like sex and race to polling worker demeanor, we next tested to see if the perceived rudeness of an election administrator might enhance a polling place wait's deleterious effect. To investigate the possibility that our (mostly Southern) mock voters had a stronger affinity for our two Southern administrators,[2] which might have lowered their stress levels, we repeated our comparison of mean stress and conformity levels for waiting and non-waiting voters facing administrators with different demeanors (hypothesis 5.2d). As shown in Table 7.7, our mock voters, whether they waited or not, showed the same tendencies when they dealt with Southern administrators. Contrary to our expectations, those facing a Southerner reported lower overall stress levels. When it comes to voting conformity, however, the findings become more variegated. The non-waiting segment of our mock electorate consistently showed equal or higher voting consistency levels when they dealt with a Southern mock election worker. In contrast, those voters who were made to wait by a Southerner exhibited lower voting conformity on half of the ballot measures. This tendency appeared when the subjects voted on two of the three more easily worded proposals but only appeared when they voted on one of the more difficultly stated ones. This again suggests that the compounded effects of polling place barriers may indeed to lead trouble in the voting booth. As before, our analyses reveal mixed support, suggesting that while polling place wait times might occasionally be troublesome for some voters, they might not be a universal ill; even when polling place experience is taken into account.

As one last test of the conditioning effect that voter commitment might have on provisional ballot use, we examined the ways in which familiarity with voting and a strong desire to cast a ballot might alleviate waiting's effect on both voter stress and voting behavior (hypotheses 6.1 and 6.2). We return to our use of correlation coefficients ranging from -1 to $+1$, correlating the frequency with which each subject reported voting in past elections on a six-point scale (ranging from "never" to "every election") and how important each subject felt voting to be on a four-point scale (from "not at all important" to "very important") with reported stress and observed voting conformity. Regarding reported stress levels, the results reported in Table 7.8 somewhat support our expectation; more frequent voters reported lower stress levels than less frequent voters. Importantly for our examination of polling place wait times, the relationship between overall stress level and the effect of having previous voting experience was stronger among those who were made to wait than among the non-waiting portion of our sample. That is, the

Table 7.8 Experience, Desire, and Poll Place Waiting

	Stress	Easy Ballot Wording			Difficult Ballot Wording		
		Marriage	Abortion	Marijuana	Marriage	Abortion	Marijuana
Non-Provisional Voters							
Frequent Voter	-0.006	-0.101	0.066	-0.038	-0.142**	0.155**	-0.085
Voting Important	-0.061	-0.204***	-0.118	-0.023	-0.031	-0.142**	-0.004
Provisional Voters							
Frequent Voter	-0.131	-0.063	0.067	-0.028	-0.069	0.080	0.022
Voting Important	-0.128	0.031	0.091	-0.138	0.046	-0.079	0.039

Notes: Cell entries are bivariate correlation coefficients. ***p<0.01, **p<0.05 (two-tailed)

impact that familiarity with the voting process had on lessening stress levels appeared to be stronger when we asked our subjects to wait. Unfortunately, these lower anxiety levels did not consistently translate into a better ability to cast conforming votes. Among both waiting and non-waiting mock voters, those voters with a longer history of electoral participation showed a tendency to cast more consistent ballots on half of the proposed amendments or less, and ballot language difficulty seemed to play a haphazard role, as well. Overall, these results suggest that a familiarity with Election Day procedures might lessen voter anxiety, but it might not be enough to ensure that voters cast ballots in the manner they intended.

Finally, we investigated the potential impact that a strong desire to cast a ballot might have by testing to see if mock voters who felt that voting was more important reported less stress and were better able to vote in a manner that reflected their opinions. As with more frequent voters, we see (in Table 7.8) that those who viewed voting as more important reported feeling less stress. Again, while this is true of both waiting and non-waiting subjects, the relationship between perceived voting importance and reported stress was stronger among the waiting segment of our mock electorate. And, importantly, our waiting mock voters' voting behavior reflected the lessened anxiety that they reported feeling. On two out of three ballot measures, these voters were better able to cast conforming votes when they felt that voting was important. Moreover, the effect was the same whether they faced more or less complicated ballot language. The same cannot be said of our non-waiting subjects; on both simple and complex ballot measures, those who felt that voting was important and experienced no wait showed a tendency to vote in a way that contradicted their previously stated preferences. Taken together, these findings suggest, somewhat perversely, that some polling place wait time might serve to focus voter attention on the importance of ballot casting and lead to better decision-making in the voting booth.

DISCUSSION

In this chapter, we explored the possible role that some election administrator and voter characteristics might play in regulating provisional ballot use and polling place wait time effects. Our results suggest that these factors had a slightly stronger effect when it came to affecting the ways in which polling place waiting affects our mock voters than they did on voters who used provisional ballots. Additionally, administrator effects tended to have more impact on the overall levels of stress reported by our provisional mock voters than they did on the voters' ability to cast votes that consistently reflected their policy preferences, while voter commitment to the electoral process showed effects on both stress and voting conformity. The conditioning effects of poll worker and voter characteristics showed a more consistent impact on our mock voters who were made to wait, most often affecting their stress levels and their ability to vote in a conforming manner.

Our expectations about the ways in which provisional voting would more greatly hamper the younger and minority members of our mock electorate were largely unsupported. Provisional voter age showed a mixed relationship with both reported stress levels and voting behavior. Similarly, while minority provisional voters reported more stress than others, they did not show a tendency to vote in a less consistent manner. The administrator characteristics we studied offer mixed support for our expectations, at best; provisional voters who encountered a minority or female poll worker did report high stress levels but did not report any distinct tendencies in their voting behavior, and our expectations about racial similarity between voters and election administrators was generally contradicted. Finally, the results with regard to administrator demeanor showed only marginal support for our expectations.

Voter demographics and administrator characteristics appeared to play a larger role when it came to polling place wait times; younger voters who were asked to wait reported higher stress levels and were less able to vote in a consistent manner on the ballot measures stated in the easiest language. We also found that minority mock voters who were asked to wait reported more stress and lower voting consistency on some proposals, although these results were less definitive. The modifying effects of polling place administrator characteristics showed more impact. While subjects who were asked by a minority poll worker to wait reported more overall stress, they did not struggle more to cast ballots in support of their preferred policies. Yet, at the same time, our expectation that mock voters asked by an election official of the same race to wait reported less stress and showed a better ability to cast conforming votes on most of the ballot proposals. Similarly, when female poll workers made members of our mock electorate wait, the voters were less likely to vote their preferences on the complexly stated ballot items. These findings illustrate the compound effects that polling place barriers might have. The combination of a female poll worker, a polling place wait, and complicated ballot language was associated with an inability to cast votes as intended. Finally, the soothing effect of a Southern demeanor that we expected were not readily evident when it came to polling place wait times; those asked to wait by a Southern poll worker reported higher stress and were able to vote more consistently on only half of the proposed amendments.

We found more support for our expectations when we examined the ways in which voter commitment might provide voters with mental tools to overcome polling place barriers. More experienced voters who were asked to either vote provisionally or wait before voting reported lower stress levels than their less experienced counterparts. Importantly, however, these subjects did not exhibit a sustained ability to cast conforming votes. Finally, the data on voter perceptions about the importance of voting revealed more consistent effects. Interestingly, but contrary to our expectation, provisional voters who felt that voting was highly important reported higher stress levels and were less able to cast ballots supporting their stated preferences. It appears that being told that one's vote may not count can cause committed voters to become angry and distracted, and our results suggest that this added angst might lead to mistakes in the voting booth. In contrast, subjects experiencing a wait showed lower stress levels and a better ability to vote consistently if they saw the act of voting as more important. Taken together, these findings suggest that voters may be able to overcome the annoyance of a lengthy polling place as long as they feel that they will eventually be able to cast their vote, but being told that their votes may not count flusters them.

NOTES

1. Though we also expect other socioeconomic indicators such as income to play a role in the effects of provisional ballot use, our data do not contain a measure of subject income. Further, the members of our sample (currently enrolled SHSU students) likely share a similar modest socioeconomic background.

2. Our Southern administrators and our minority administrators included both genders.

Chapter 8

Dealing with Polling Place Stressors

Conclusions and Implications

Our goal in this book was to look at the stress recent polling place barriers place on voters and the ways in which such stress might relate to behavior inside the voting booth. Our findings provided mixed support for this proposition (and hypothesis 1), with different types of barriers affecting participation and vote choice in different ways. Our study of mock voters revealed that complicated ballot language continues to trouble voters (supporting hypothesis 4). At the same time, our investigation of the effects of long wait times at the polling place and especially provisional ballots met with less support. Our mock provisional voters reported lower stress levels and proved better able to cast ballots conforming to their earlier stated preferences than did those subjects who were allowed to vote non-provisionally (providing mixed support for hypotheses 2 and 3). And while polling place wait times and the stress accompanying them was associated with an impaired ability to cast ballots in ways supportive of previously stated voter preferences, the predicted effects proved to be minor (providing some support for hypotheses 2 and 3). Taken together, the findings with regard to provisional balloting and, sometimes, polling place wait times speak to voters' resiliency in the face of stressors such as provisional ballots and frustrating waits at the polling place.

When faced with more complex ballot language, our mock voters showed a marked tendency to cast more incomplete ballots and to vote in a manner that did not accurately reflect their previously stated preferences; this pattern held across racial and partisan lines as well as among those voters with various levels of political knowledge and voting experience. When confronted with complex ballot language (whether in combination with other polling place barriers or not), our mock voters participated at lower rates and voted less consistently, with only one exception—the issue of legalized marijuana. This issue, however, was stated in simpler ballot language, relative to the other issues. Even the more complexly worded marijuana legalization measure had a relatively low Flesch-Kinkaid readability score. The higher voting conformity levels exhibited by our mock voters on this issue might well support the argument that more easily worded ballot measures present less of a challenge to voters. On the whole, more complex ballot language appears to complicate the act of voting in ways that lead to significantly higher levels of inconsistent voting. Both the nature and significance of our findings suggests that ballot language complexity represents a potential voting barrier that election officials might be well advised to address.

Our investigation of provisional ballot use resulted in unsupportive, and even contradictory, findings. Our mock provisional voters expressed anxiety and exhibited higher levels of consistent voting. Provisional ballots, it seems, had a calming effect on our mock voters and did not complicate their decision-making when they cast their ballots. Participants in our study were able to overcome the stress of having their voting rights challenged and voted consistently with their policy preferences on the ballot propositions. Thus, while participants were uncertain of being able to participate or of having their ballot counted, they took the process seriously and pushed through the obstacles to make good decisions in the mock ballot booth. The contradictory findings that emerged suggest that voters in actual elections might be able to capably overcome this barrier when it is placed in their electoral path. Perhaps the uproar over provisional ballot use constitutes an outcry "full of sound and fury, signifying nothing" (with apologies to Lord Macbeth; Shakespeare 2013, 5.5, 30–31).

Our findings with regard to polling place wait times offer somewhat supportive evidence for our premise. Mock voters who were made to wait reported more stressful voting experiences, but this added stress was only sometimes associated with a lowered ability to cast a ballot in support of previously expressed positions. And even when voting consistency was impaired, the effects were typically extremely small and inconsistent across topics or amendments. Most likely, then, a lengthy polling place wait would cause voters to fret but would only impair voting on some issues some of the time. Importantly, though, these effects are slightly higher for minority participants.

Even though some polling place barriers may be inconvenient and unsupportive of increased participation, this does not mean that they should be completely ignored. Our findings regarding the ways in which these obstacles impact different segments of the electorate suggest that some barriers' disenfranchising effects may not be uniform. While many voters might not be much affected by them, some voters' willingness and/or ability to cast meaningful ballots could be greatly impaired. Furthermore, a combination of polling place obstacles could cause trouble for even more voters; when complex ballot language compounds provisional voting and/or lengthy waiting times, even more voters could be adversely affected.

Add unfamiliar or nuanced issue topics to this electoral mire, and voters face even more difficulty. Our mock voters had more trouble with some issues than others; on issues made salient by the current political atmosphere, voters may be more able to overcome the polling place stressors they encounter. Polling place stressors, however, can more easily obstruct voter intent on issues that may not be central in the campaign context. On the whole, then, our results speak directly to concerns about the polling place obstacles of ballot design, registration problems and their consequences, and poll worker training that have been brought to light in recent elections. Furthermore, the sex, race, and demeanor of the poll workers, especially in combination with other obstacles, can further contribute to both voters' stress levels and their ability to conform to their policy preferences (consistent with hypotheses 5 and 6).

KEEPING THINGS IN PERSPECTIVE

While experimental studies have many strengths, some important shortcomings accompanying them impact the degree to which findings from an experiment should be generalized. Our relatively small sample size represents one common experimental shortcoming. Unlike survey researchers in the field, who typically interview a thousand or more respondents, we studied three groups of mock voters comprised of about a hundred voters per group. Experimental researchers, including this study's authors, must face the fact that smaller sample sizes result in higher sampling error levels, which works against statistically significant findings. While the findings presented here are suggestive, our results' insignificance calls for caution when speaking about potential causality and effect magnitude. As our earlier primer on statistical methods pointed out, statistically insignificant findings indicate that the many of the findings from our sample should not be generalized too far.

Furthermore, the representativeness of the sample suggests that these results should not be overly generalized. Though our sample was racially and ethnically diverse, it was still largely comprised of traditionally aged college students. While our sample was likely representative of the young voter population, we must be careful not to assume that the older segments of the electorate would perform in a similar manner. Our results with regard to the minimal effects that polling place wait times had on voting conformity offer one example of how our college student sample might differ from the general public. Perhaps our participants, who were likely accustomed to waiting at various academic and administrative offices across campus, were not as perturbed by wait times as older members of the electorate might be. Similarly, we must remain cognizant of the differences between voters with some college education and those with less formal education, as well as the differences between the ways in which younger, millennial generation voters react to interpersonal exchanges as opposed to their reactions to more distant electronic forms of communication.

Some might also question whether the different voting formats for our provisional mock voters and others could be playing some role in the results; it is possible that some of the weak findings with regard to this obstacle might be a result of our provisional voters having to cast paper ballots, while nonprovisional voters cast ballots electronically. While this possibility limits our ability to speak to provisional ballots' impact, it offers an exciting opportunity to explore the possible differences between electronic and paper ballot mechanisms.

As always, we must recognize the unique political context within which this study was conducted. The 2016 primary election, even in a typically noncompetitive state such as Texas, offered primary races within both parties that captured the public's attention more than most. The galvanizing candidacies of Donald Trump and Hillary Clinton, along with the appeal that Bernie Sanders held for many college-age voters and the presence of a Texas senator in the primary contests, likely heightened both our mock voters' interest in the electoral process and their commitment to voting, factors that our and others' analyses have shown to affect voting behavior.

Furthermore, as with any study, this study had measurement shortcomings that must be kept in mind: in making the coding decision for our voting conformity measures, it is possible that we have masked some important variation in this variable. Future studies might explore alternative ways of coding the pretest ten-point preference scale to compare the dichotomous posttest mock vote. Similarly, a closer investigation of the ways in which particular items in the stress index might relate to wait times and voting conformity could prove insightful. Given our findings with regard to election administrator characteristics, exploring the correlates of negative feelings about polling place interpersonal interactions might offer fruitful information.

FUTURE INVESTIGATIONS

The landscape of voting rights and potential challenges to those rights continues to change. A plethora of recent court decisions suggests that debate about these issues will continue for the foreseeable future.[1] While we have studied the impact of some of the factors at issue in recent court cases, there are many other studies yet to be conducted, such as a more focused analysis of the ways in which long polling place wait times place a burden on voters of different ages. At the same time, there might be additional insight to be gained by studying our college-age sample. For instance, we believe that non-native English speakers might experience more stress and have more difficulty navigating a ballot written entirely in English. A follow-up study investigating the ways in which polling place barriers might cause non-native English speakers more difficulty than other groups could inform arguments about requirements involving non-English-language ballots.

We would also like to test the effect of the time that elapsed between the respondents' pretest statement of preferences and their participation in the mock election, with the expectation that those voters who waited a longer time between completing the online pretest and participating in the mock election might exhibit lower voting conformity. Similarly, we would like to leverage a second measure of pretest preferences by exploring the possibility that those choosing more than one policy option from a list in the pretest might exhibit less voting conformity when faced with the blunt instrument of a dichotomous vote choice.

WHAT'S NEXT FOR THE STATES? POLICY IMPLICATIONS

Clearly, one of the most pressing difficulties voters face is the ability to read and understand the ballot. Ballot readability has an overarching effect on both participation and quality of participation, regardless of other obstacles voters encounter. Given the strong influence ballot language exerted, state governments might want to address such problems with further policy reforms. As our results suggest, ballot content can exert a substantial impact on voter participation quality. In fact, both the 2000 and 2016 presidential elections produced concerns about ballot design decisions potentially leading voters to mistakenly cast ballots supporting candidates they did not prefer. The HAVA introduced a number of modifications aimed at increasing voters' ability to vote consistently with their policy preferences, and states could support these efforts by working to institute consistent ballot language regulations. Some states regulate ballot measure language by suggesting that the language be succinct and straightforward, and some states put length limitations and topic restrictions on ballot language, but no states have a comprehensive plan to ensure that voters can read and understand the measures put before them (Reilly 2010, 2015). While our project included measures from statewide races, there are also ballot measures on the local level that are subject to even fewer regulations. Readability is just one aspect of ballot accessibility, but it is a relatively simple test that could be conducted to evaluate the ease with which voters are able to understand ballot content. Should a ballot measure prove to be overly complex, simple limitations, such as limiting the number of words in the passage, could help remove the barrier of complicated ballot language from voters' paths (Reilly 2010; Reilly and Richey 2011; Magebly 1980).

Furthermore, polling place quality (Barreto, Cohen-Marks, and Woods 2009; DeWitt et al. 2005) encompasses a number of factors that contribute to voters' willingness to participate. Just as our study showed that voter experiences at the polling place can affect their willingness and ability to cast a ballot, other factors, such as parking availability, convenient bus routes, building accessibility, lighting conditions, and sufficient voting machines might prove as important as ballot design.

On the whole, our findings suggest that steps such as the ones enumerated in this study can help make the polling place a less daunting place for many voters. Perhaps focused attention to finding solutions to the factors contributing to the polling place pandemonium and confusion that have been highlighted in recent elections could help create a less stressful polling place atmosphere that does not hinder either the willingness or the ability of voters to accurately express their preferences in the voting booth.

NOTE

1. A sampling of recent cases on voting issues: gerrymandering (e.g., *Vieth vs. Jubelirer; Arizona State Legislature v. Arizona Independent Redistricting Commission; Gill vs. Whitford*), voter identification (e.g., *Texas NAACP vs. Steen, North Carolina vs. North Carolina State Conference of the NAACP, Crawford v. Marion County Election Board*), early voting (e.g., *League of Women Voters of North Carolina vs. Howard, NAACP vs. Husted, Obama for America vs. Husted* and voting machines (e.g., *Gusciora vs. Christie, Banfield vs. Aichele, Banfield vs. Cortes*).

Appendix A

Subject Recruitment

We used a number of different methods to recruit a representative sample of subjects for this study. At the beginning of the spring 2016 semester, we contacted all Sam Houston State University (SHSU) faculty members teaching required introductory courses in history, sociology, and political science classes, described the study to them and asked if they would help recruit students from their classes to participate. Nineteen different faculty members teaching more than 2,000 students volunteered to help inform students of the opportunity to participate in the study. Faculty members were allowed, but not required, to offer class credit for participation.

We then worked with a graphic designer to develop a website and study announcement. The announcement, shown in Figure A.1, invited those in the campus community "to participate in a voluntary election study about [their] policy positions on topics such as abortion, gay marriage, etc." in exchange for the possibility of winning one of twenty $10 Starbuck gift cards for completing the first part of the study (the online survey) and the possibility of winning one of fifteen $20 Starbucks gift cards for participation in the second part of the study (the mock election). Those interested in participating were directed to the online survey, which became available to participants on February 8, 2016.

The study website (see Figure A.2) explained the purpose of the study, provided subjects with a web link to the online survey that served as the first part of the study, and reminded them of their eligibility to win a $10 gift card for completing the survey. The website became available on February 8 and remained available until February 25.

On February 5, 2016, we emailed all participating faculty providing them with the link to the study website and a copy of the study announcement (shown in Figure A.1), asking them to distribute both items to the students

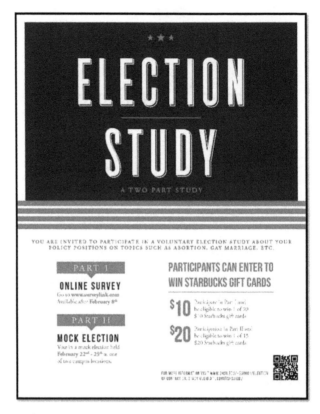

Figure A.1   Study Announcement.

in their classes. At the same time, we posted the study announcement on bulletin boards in academic and recreational buildings across the Sam Houston State University campus. Additionally, we placed small handbills announcing the study on tables in the food courts, library study areas, and residence hall lobbies on campus.

The recruitment and participation of subjects was approved by the Internal Review Boards (IRBs) of both Sam Houston State University and Northern Kentucky University. Per IRB requirements, all study participants were informed of their rights as research subjects and asked to consent to participation in the study before taking part in it.

Figure A.2 Study Website.

Appendix B

Pretest Survey

(Administered Online)

Party Identification: Which political party do you usually support?

1. Democratic Party
2. Republican Party
3. Other: _____
4. Independent
5. Don't know

Ideology: Do you consider yourself politically conservative or liberal?

1. Conservative
2. Liberal

How strongly do you align yourself with this ideology; would you say you are a:

1. Strong conservative
2. Moderate conservative
3. Leaning conservative
4. Independent
5. Leaning liberal
6. Moderate liberal
7. Strong liberal

Personal Information:
Gender: Male Female
Year you were born: _____

Race: _____
Citizen Attributions: (circle the answer you feel best describes your opinion)
How sophisticated are citizens in terms of policy?

a. Very Sophisticated
b. Good on some issues
c. Usually unqualified
d. Unsophisticated

Voting
Assuming you could vote in the last Presidential election would you have voted?

a. Yes
b. No

Who would you have voted for?

a. Obama
b. Romney
c. Other (specify) _____

If you did, in fact, vote, how long did you wait to vote?

a. Less than twenty minutes
b. Half an hour
c. One hour
d. An hour and a half
e. Two hours
f. More than 2 hours

How long would you have waited to vote?

a. Less than twenty minutes
b. Half an hour
c. One hour
d. An hour and a half
e. Two hours
f. More than two hours

How important is voting to you personally?

a. Very important
b. Somewhat important
c. Occasionally important
d. Somewhat unimportant
e. Not at all important

How many times have you voted in the past?

a. Never
b. Once, the last election was my first time voting
c. Twice
d. More than two times, but I usually don't vote
e. I vote in most elections
f. I vote in every election

How involved are you in your community?

a. Not at all involved
b. Not very involved
c. Somewhat involved
d. Very involved

How interested are you in politics?

a. Not at all interested
b. Not very interested
c. Somewhat interested
d. Very interested

How knowledgeable are you about politics?

a. Not at all knowledgeable
b. Not very knowledgeable
c. Somewhat knowledgeable
d. Very knowledgeable

Political questions: (Fill in the answers on the blanks below)
What job or political office is now held by Joseph Biden?
_____

Whose responsibility is it to determine if a law is constitutional or not ... .
Is it the President, the Congress or the Supreme Court? _____

How much of a majority is required for the US Senate and House to override a presidential veto? _____

Do you happen to know which party currently has the most members in the House of Representatives in Washington? _____

Would you say that one of the parties is more conservative than the other at the national level? Which party is more conservative? _____

Opinion Questions

There has been some discussion about allowing Washington, D.C. to become the 51st state in recent years. Below is a short list of opinions. Click, or circle, *each* opinion with which you AGREE:

1. Washington, D.C. should not be admitted as a state.
2. Washington, D.C. should not be admitted as a state, unless a constitutional amendment is passed changing its status.
3. Washington, D.C. should not be admitted as a state, unless the change is approved by a majority of the residents of the city, and approved by a vote in Congress.
4. Washington D.C. should be admitted as a state, but the US Government should establish a new capital city, in a territory not contained within the existing states.
5. Washington D.C. should be admitted as a state.

There has been some discussion about abortion in recent years. Below is a short list of opinions. Click, or circle, *each* opinion with which you AGREE:

1. Abortion should be illegal.
2. Abortion should be illegal, but not in cases of rape or incest.
3. Abortion should be illegal, but not the woman's life is in danger
4. Under normal circumstances, a woman should be required to meet with a physician to receive information about the abortion procedure and its risks before an abortion procedure.
5. Doctors providing abortion services should have to submit reports to the state summarizing how abortion information was given to patients, and the state should make summaries of that information available to the public.
6. The decision to have an abortion should be between a woman and her doctor, and the state should not be involved in that decision.
7. Abortion should be legal.

There has been some discussion about same-sex marriage in recent years. Below is a short list of opinions. Click, or circle, *each* opinion with which you AGREE:

1. Only marriages between one man and one woman should be legal.
2. States should be allowed to not recognize same-sex marriages performed in other states or countries.
3. Same-sex couples should be allowed to form Domestic Partnerships, but should not be allowed to get married.
4. Same-sex domestic partners should receive the same treatment as married couples when it comes to legal benefits, rights, and responsibilities.
5. Same-sex couples should be allowed to get married.

There has been some discussion about legalizing the use of marijuana in recent years. Below is a short list of opinions. Click, or circle, *each* opinion with which you AGREE:

1. Marijuana use should be illegal.
2. Marijuana use should be illegal, except in cases when it is prescribed by a doctor.
3. Marijuana use should be illegal, unless the user is on a confidential list of authorized patients, maintained by the state.
4. Marijuana use should be legal, but its sale should be regulated by the state.
5. Marijuana use should be legal, but it should be taxed by the state.
6. Marijuana use should be legal, but its misuse (such as by driving under its influence) should be punished by the state.
7. Marijuana use should be legal.

There has been some discussion about gun control in recent years. Below is a short list of opinions. Click, or circle, *each* opinion with which you AGREE:

1. Gun ownership should be illegal, except in the cases of law enforcement or military service personnel.
2. Gun ownership should be illegal, unless a citizen has training and a license allowing him or her to own a gun.
3. Gun ownership should be legal, but states can require criminal background checks and prohibit convicted criminals from owning a gun.
4. Gun ownership should be legal, but the government should keep a confidential list of gun owners.
5. Gun ownership should be legal.

Rate your agreement with the following statements from 1 (strongly disagree) to 10 (strongly agree).

Washington, D.C. should be admitted to the United States as a state.

1 2 3 4 5 6 7 8 9 10 N/A

Medical abortion should be safe and legal in this state.
1 2 3 4 5 6 7 8 9 10 N/A
There should be legally sanctioned gay marriage allowed in this state.
1 2 3 4 5 6 7 8 9 10 N/A
Marijuana should be legal in this state.
1 2 3 4 5 6 7 8 9 10 N/A
Same-sex partners should be allowed to marry in this state.
1 2 3 4 5 6 7 8 9 10 N/A
Citizens of this state should be allowed to buy and sell firearms without government interference.
1 2 3 4 5 6 7 8 9 10 N/A
Issue Importance
Of the following issues circle the answer that best describes how important that issue is to you personally
As an issue, Washington D.C. statehood is:

a.   Not important to me
b.   Somewhat important to me
c.   Very important to me

As an issue, gay marriage is:

a.   Not important to me
b.   Somewhat important to me
c.   Very important to me

As an issue, the legalization of marijuana is

a.   Not important to me
b.   Somewhat important to me
c.   Very important to me

As an issue, abortion is:

a.   Not important to me
b.   Somewhat important to me
c.   Very important to me

As an issue, gun control is:

a.   Not important to me
b.   Somewhat important to me
c.   Very important to me

Appendix C

Posttest, Mock Election Ballot

Amendment No. 1: This proposed constitutional amendment provides that marriage may take place and may be valid under the laws of this state only between a man and a woman.

The amendment also provides that a marriage in another state or foreign jurisdiction between persons of the same gender may not be recognized in this state and is void and unenforceable under the laws of this state.

Yes

No

No Vote

Amendment No. 2: Do you want to ban a specific abortion procedure to be defined in law, except in cases where the life of the mother is in danger?

Yes

No

No Vote

Amendment No. 3

Title: Bill allowing medical use of marijuana

Summary: This bill would allow patients to use marijuana for certain medical purposes. A doctor must find that the patient has a debilitating medical condition that might benefit from marijuana. An eligible minor could use medical marijuana only under the consent and control of a parent. There would be limits on how much medical marijuana a patient could possess. Patients and their primary care-givers who comply with this law would not be guilty of a crime. The state would create a confidential registry of patients who may use medical marijuana. Non-medical use of marijuana would still be a crime.

Should this initiative become law?

Yes

No
No Vote
Amendment No. 4
Title: Domestic Partnerships
Summary: Shall there be an amendment to the Texas Revised Statutes to authorize domestic partnerships, an in connection therewith, enacting the "Texas Domestic Partnership Benefits and Responsibilities Act" to extend to same-sex couples in a domestic partnership the benefits, protections, and responsibilities that are granted by Texas law to spouses, providing the conditions under which a license for a domestic partnership may be issued and the criteria under which a domestic partnership may be dissolved, making provisions for implementation of the Act, and providing that a domestic partnership is not a marriage, which consists of the union of one man and one woman?
Yes
No
No Vote
Amendment No. 5
Shall there be an amendment to the Texas Revised Statutes concerning the requirement that any woman who is considering an abortion give voluntary, informed consent prior to the abortion, and, in connection therewith, defining several pertinent terms so that "abortion" includes termination of a known pregnancy at any time after conception, specifying the information a physician must provide to insure that a woman's consent to an abortion is voluntary and informed, requiring a physician, except in emergency cases, to provide the specified information to the woman at least twenty-four hours prior to performing an abortion, requiring the department of public health and environment to provide specified informational materials for women who are considering abortions, establishing procedures for emergency situations, requiring physicians to annually report specified information, requiring the department of public health and environment to annually publish a compilation of the physicians' reports, and providing for the administration and enforcement of the amendment's provisions?
Yes
No
No Vote
Amendment No. 6
Title: Regulation of Marijuana
Summary: Shall Titles 32, 40, and 43 of the Texas Revised Statutes be amended in order to allow and regulate the sale, use, and possession of one ounce or less of marijuana by persons at least 21 years of age; impose licensing requirements on marijuana retailers and wholesalers; allow for the sale of

marijuana by licensed marijuana retailers and wholesalers; impose taxes and restrictions on the wholesale and retail sale of marijuana; and to increase the criminal penalties for causing death or substantial bodily harm when driving while under the influence of drugs or alcohol?

Yes

No

No Vote

Assuming you could vote in the *upcoming Texas presidential primary*, how would you vote?

Republican

Democrat

Other

Specify *which candidate* within that party: _____

Below are listed a variety of events that may be viewed as stressful or unpleasant. Read each item carefully and decide whether or not that event occurred during this experiment. Indicate if the event occurred and if it did, indicate the amount of stress that it caused you. Please answer as honestly as you can so that we may obtain accurate information.

0 = did not occur (while waiting in line)

1 = occurred but was not stressful

2 = caused very little stress

3 = caused a little stress

4 = caused some stress

5 = caused much stress

6 = caused very much stress

7 = caused me to panic

Thought about unfinished work

Hurried to meet deadline

Interrupted during task/activity

Someone spoiled your completed task

Criticized or verbally attacked

Dealt with rude person

Interrupted while talking

Was forced to socialize

Someone broke a promise/appointment

Was stared at

Experienced unwanted physical contact

(crowded, pushed)

Was misunderstood

Thought about the future

Waiting longer than you wanted

Someone "cut" ahead of you in a line

Did something that you did not want to do

Measures, Coding, and Distribution of Responses

Voting Conformity: Based on a comparison of responses to the pre- and post-test questions below. 1 = respondent's pre-test response conformed with the post-test response; 0 = respondent's pre-test response did not conform with the post-test response. Respondents choosing in the "Neither Agree/ Disagree" on the pre-test or choosing "no vote" (or not responding) on the post-test were coded as missing cases and excluded from analysis.

Pre-test (Online Survey): "Rate your agreement with the following statements from 1 (strongly disagree) to 10 (strongly agree)."

Same-sex Marriage Referendum: "There should be legally sanctioned gay marriage allowed in this state."
Abortion Referendum: "Medical abortion should be safe and legal in this state."
Marijuana Referendum: "Marijuana should be legal in this state."

Post-Test (Mock Ballot): "Please vote for the following six amendments—'Yes' to adopt the measure, 'No' to keep the current policy, you may also choose 'No Vote' to skip the question." 1 = Yes; 2 = No; 3 = No Vote.

Same-sex Marriage Referendum (Easy Ballot Language): "Amendment No. 1 This proposed constitutional amendment provides that marriage may take place and may be valid under the laws of this state only between a man and a woman. The amendment also provides that a marriage in another state or foreign jurisdiction between persons of the same gender may not be recognized in this state and is void and unenforceable under the laws of this state."
Respondents choosing values 0 to 4 ("disagree") in the pre-test and "yes" (1) in the post-test or choosing values 6 to 10 ("agree") in the pre-test and "no" (2) in the post-test are coded as conforming.
Abortion Referendum (Easy Ballot Language): "Amendment No. 2 Do you want

to ban a specific abortion procedure to be defined in law, except in cases where the life of the mother is in danger?"

Respondents choosing values 0 to 4 ("disagree") in the pre-test and "yes" (1) in the post-test or choosing values 6 to 10 ("agree") in the pre-test and "no" (2) in the post-test are coded as conforming.

Marijuana Referendum (Easy Ballot Language): "Amendment No. 3 Title: Bill allowing medical use of marijuana. Summary: This bill would allow patients to use marijuana for certain medical purposes. A doctor must find that the patient has a debilitating medical condition that might benefit from marijuana. An eligible minor could use medical marijuana only under the consent and control of a parent. There would be limits on how much medical marijuana a patient could possess. Patients and their primary care-givers who comply with this law would not be guilty of a crime. The state would create a confidential registry of patients who may use medical marijuana. Non-medical use of marijuana would still be a crime. Should this initiative become law?"

Respondents choosing values 0 to 4 ("disagree") in the pre-test and "no" (2) in the post-test or choosing values 6 to 10 ("agree") in the pre-test and "yes" (1) in the post-test are coded as conforming.

Same-sex Marriage Referendum (Difficult Ballot Language): "Amendment No. 4. Title: Domestic Partnerships. Summary: Shall there be an amendment to the Texas Revised Statutes to authorize domestic partnerships, an in connection therewith, enacting the "Texas Domestic Partnership Benefits and Responsibilities Act" to extend to same-sex couples in a domestic partnership the benefits, protections, and responsibilities that are granted by Texas law to spouses, providing the conditions under which a license for a domestic partnership may be issued and the criteria under which a domestic partnership may be dissolved, making provisions for implementation of the Act, and providing that a domestic partnership is not a marriage, which consists of the union of one man and one woman?

Respondents choosing values 0 to 4 ("disagree") in the pre-test and "no" (2) in the post-test or choosing values 6 to 10 ("agree") in the pre-test and "yes" (1) in the post-test are coded as conforming.

Abortion Referendum (Difficult Ballot Language): "Amendment No. 5. Shall there be an amendment to the Texas Revised Statutes concerning the requirement that any woman who is considering an abortion give voluntary, informed consent prior to the abortion, and, in connection therewith, defining several pertinent terms so that "abortion" includes termination of a known pregnancy at any time after conception, specifying the information a physician must provide to insure that a woman's consent to an abortion is voluntary and informed, requiring a physician, except in emergency cases, to provide the specified information to the woman at least twenty-four hours prior to performing an abortion, requiring the department of public health and environment to provide specified informational materials for women who are considering abortions, establishing procedures for emergency situations, requiring physicians to annually report specified information, requiring the department of public health and environment to annually publish a compilation of the physicians' reports, and providing for the administration and enforcement of the amendment's provisions?"

Respondents choosing values 0 to 4 ("disagree") in the pre-test and "yes" (1) in the post-test or choosing values 6 to 10 ("agree") in the pre-test and "no" (2) in the post-test are coded as conforming.

Marijuana Referendum (Difficult Ballot Language): "Amendment No. 6. Title: Regulation of Marijuana Summary: Shall Titles 32, 40 and 43 of the Texas Revised Statutes be amended in order to allow and regulate the sale, use and possession of one ounce or less of marijuana by persons at least 21 years of age, impose licensing requirements on marijuana retailers and wholesalers, allow for the sale of marijuana by licensed marijuana retailers and wholesalers, impose taxes and restrictions on the wholesale and retail sale of marijuana, and to increase the criminal penalties for causing death or substantial bodily harm when driving while under the influence of drugs or alcohol?"

Respondents choosing values 0 to 4 ("disagree") in the pre-test and "no" (2) in the post-test or choosing values 6 to 10 ("agree") in the pre-test and "yes" (1) in the post-test are coded as conforming.

Ballot Complexity: Based on the Flesch-Kincaid Grade Level index to measure the level of education required to read and comprehend each ballot referenda. Index calculated using the average sentence length (ASL) and average number of syllables per word (ASW) according to the following formula: $(.39 \times ASL) + (11.8 \times ASW) - 15.59$ (Kincaid et al. 1975). We designate the three ballot measures with the lowest Flesch-Kincaid index score as "easy" ballot issues while we consider the three with the highest scores "difficult."

Provisional Ballot: Whether the respondent was required to vote via a paper, provisional ballot (coded 1) or not (coded 0).

Wait Time: Elapsed time, in minutes, between subject speaking with polling place administrator and allowed to begin voting. Mean: 10.84; std.dev.: 3.65; median: 10; range: 0–24.

Stress: Six-point scale calculated by taking each subject's mean self-placement on 16 potentially stressful events (see question wording below). Question asked in post-test. Mean: 1.12; std.dev.: 1.27; median: 0.56; range: 0–4.44.

"Below are listed a variety of events that may be viewed as stressful or unpleasant. Read each item carefully and decide whether or not that event occurred during this experiment. If the event *did not occur*, place an "X" in the space next to that item. If the event *did occur*, indicate the amount of stress that it caused you by placing a number from 1 to 7 in the space next to that item (see numbers below). Please answer as honestly as you can so that we may obtain accurate information." 0 = did not occur (while waiting in line); 0 = occurred but was not stressful; 1 = caused very little stress; 2 = caused a little stress; 3 = caused some stress; 4 = caused much stress; 5 = caused very much stress; 6 = caused me to panic.

 1. Thought about unfinished work
 2. Hurried to meet deadline
 3. Interrupted during task/activity
 4. Someone spoiled your completed task
 5. Criticized or verbally attacked
 6. Dealt with rude person
 7. Interrupted while talking
 8. Was forced to socialize
 9. Someone broke a promise/appointment
10. Was stared at
11. Experienced unwanted physical contact (crowded, pushed)
12. Was misunderstood
13. Thought about the future
14. Waiting longer than you wanted
15. Someone "cut" ahead of you in a line
16. Did something that you did not want to do

Political Knowledge: Each subject's mean score on four open-ended "civics quiz" style political knowledge questions (see question wording below). Question asked in pre-test. 1 = correct answer; 0 = incorrect or no answer. Mean: 0.74; std.dev.: 0.28; median: 0.80; range: 0–4.

"What job or political office is now held by Joseph Biden?

Whose responsibility is it to determine if a law is constitutional or not … . Is it the President, the Congress or the Supreme Court?

How much of a majority is required for the US Senate and House to override a presidential veto?

Do you happen to know which party currently has the most members in the House of Representatives in Washington?

Would you say that one of the parties is more conservative than the other at the national level? Which party is more conservative?"

Non-Native US Citizen: Subject's citizenship status: 0 = natural born US citizen (88%); 1 = naturalized US citizen (1%), resident alien (2%), non-resident alien (8%), unknown (1.5%). Information coded from official student registration records.

Partisan Strength: "If you identify as a Republican or a Democrat, would you say that you are a ... ." Question asked in pre-test. 1 = strong Republican/ Democrat (27.4%); 0 = not very strong Republican/Democrat (72.6%).

Ideological Strength: "Do you consider yourself politically conservative or liberal?" Question asked on pre-test. 1 = Strong conservative, Strong liberal (10.3%); 0 = Moderate conservative, Leaning conservative, Independent, Leaning liberal, Moderate liberal (89.7%)

Past Voting History: "How many times have you voted in the past?" Question asked on pre-test. 1 = Never (80.8%); Once, the last election was my first time voting (8.1%); Twice (5.1%); More than two times, but I usually don't vote (1.4%); I vote in most elections (2.7%); I vote in every election (1.9%).

View Voting as Important: "How important is voting to you personally?" Question asked on pre-test. 4 = Very important (35.8%); 3 = Somewhat important (43.4%; 2 = Just a little important (14.1%); 1 = Not at all important (6.8%).

Political Interest: "How interested are you in politics?" Question asked on pre-test. 1 = Not at all interested (12.8%); 2 = Not very interested (22.3%); 3 = Somewhat interested (48.8%); 4 = Very interested (16.1%).

Age: Subject's age in years, calculated on report year of birth. Question asked on pre-test. Mean: 21.04; std.dev.: 3.8; median: 20; range: 19–50.

Hispanic: 1 = Subject is Hispanic (22.5%); 0 = Subject is not Hispanic (77.5%). Information coded from official student registration records.

Black: 1 = Subject's race is black (19.5%); 0 = subject's race is not black (80.5%). Information coded from official student registration records.

Female: 1 = Subject self-identifies as female (68.6%); 0 = subject self-identifies as male (31.4%). Question asked in pre-test.

Bibliography

Addonizio, Elizabeth M., Donald P. Green, and James M. Glaser. 2007. "Putting the Party Back into Politics: An Experiment Testing Whether Election Day Festivals Increase Voter Turnout." *PS: Political Science and Politics* 40 (4): 721–27.

Alesina, Alberto, and Eliana La Ferrara. 2000. "Participation in Heterogeneous Communities." *Quarterly Journal of Economics* 115 (3): 847–904.

Allen, Theodore, and Mikhail Bernshteyn. 2006. "Mitigating Waiting Times." *Chance* 19 (4): 25–34.

Alvarez, R. Michael, Stephen Ansolabehere, and Charles Stewart. 2005. "Studying Elections: Data Quality and Pitfalls in Measuring of Effects of Voting Technologies." *Policy Studies Journal* 33 (1): 15–24.

Alvarez, R. Michael, Melanie Goodrich, Thad E. Hall, D. Roderick Kiewiet, and Sarah M. Sled. 2004. "The Complexity of the California Recall Election." *Political Science and Politics* 37 (1): 23–26.

Alvarez, R. Michael, and Thad E. Hall. 2006. "Controlling Democracy: The Principal–Agent Problems in Election Administration." *Policy Studies Journal* 34 (4): 491–510.

———. 2009. "Provisional Ballots in the 2008 Ohio General Elections." *The Pew Charitable Trusts*. http://www.pewtrusts.org/~/media/legacy/uploaded-files/pcs_assets/2009/provballotsalvarezhallohessay1pdf.pdf. Accessed October 23, 2017.

Anderson, Eugene W., and Mary W. Sullivan. 1993. "The Antecedents and Consequences of Customer Satisfaction for Firms." *Marketing Science* 12: 125–43.

Ansolabehere, Stephen, and Shanto Iyengar. 1995. *Going Negative: How Political Advertisements Shrink and Polarize the Electorate.* New York: Free Press.

Ansolabehere, Stephen, and Charles Stewart. 2005. "Residual Votes Attributable to Technology." *Journal of Politics* 67 (2): 365–89.

Ansolabehere, Stephen. 2007. "Access Versus Integrity in Voter Identification Requirements." *New York University Annual Survey of American Law* 63: 613.

The Arizona Republic. 2006. "Provisional Ballots in Arizona: What you need to know if you cast one, or are about to." *AZ Central*. November 8. http://www.azcentral.com/story/news/politics/elections/2016/11/08/provisional-ballots-arizona-what-you-need-know/93484498/.

Arlington, Michele. 1990. "English-Only Laws and Direct Legislation: The Battle in the States over Language Minority Rights." *Journal of Law and Politics* 7: 324.

The Associated Press. 2005. "Counting of 2004 Provisional Ballots Varied Widely, Study Finds." *The New York Times*, March 20.

Atkeson, Lonna Rae, and Kyle L. Saunders. "Voter Confidence: A Local Matter?" *PS: Political Science & Politics* 40 (4): 655–60.

Atkeson, Lonna Rae, Lisa Ann Bryant, Thad E. Hall, Kyle L. Saunders, and R. Michael Alvarez. 2010. "A New Barrier to Participation: Heterogeneous Application of Voter Identification Policies." *Electoral Studies* 29 (1): 66–73.

Austen-Smith, David, and Jeffrey S. Banks. 1996. "Information Aggregation, Rationality, and the Condorcet Jury Theorem." *The American Political Science Review* 90 (1): 34–45.

Bacon, Stephen J. 1974. "Arousal and the Range of Cue Utilization." *Journal of Experimental Psychology* 102: 81–87.

Baddeley, Alan D. 1972. "Selective Attention and Performance in Dangerous Environments." *British Journal of Psychology* 63: 537–46.

Barreto, Matt A., Mara Cohen-Marks, and Nathan D. Woods. 2009. "Are All Precincts Created Equal? The Prevalence of Low-Quality Precincts in Low-Income and Minority Communities." *Political Research Quarterly* 62 (3): 445–58.

Barreto, Matt A., and Ricardo Ramirez. 2004. "Minority Participation and the California Recall: Latino, Black, and Asian Voting Trends, 1990–2003." *PS: Political Science and Politics* 37 (1): 11–14.

Baybeck, Brady, and David Kimball. 2008. "The Political Geography of Provisional Ballots." Paper presented at the Annual Meeting of the American Political Science Association, Chicago, IL, April.

Becker, Gary S. 1965. "A Theory of the Allocation of Time." *Economic Journal* 75 (299): 493–517.

Ben-Ezra, Menachem, Yuval Palgi, G. James Rubin, Yaira Hamama-Raz, and Robin Goodwin. 2013. "The Association Between Self-Reported Change in Vote for the Presidential Election of 2012 and Posttraumatic Stress Disorder Symptoms Following Hurricane Sandy." *Psychiatry Research* 210 (3): 1304–06.

Benaloh, Josh. 2006. "Towards Simple Verifiable Elections." In *Proceedings of Workshop on Trustworthy Election*, 61–68.

Bergbower, Matthew L. 2014. "Campaign Intensity and Voting Correctly in Senate Elections." *Journal of Elections, Public Opinion and Parties* 24 (1): 90–114.

Berinsky, Adam J. 2005. "The Perverse Consequences of Electoral Reform in the United States." *American Politics Research* 33 (4): 471–91.

Bishop, George F., Alfred J. Tuchfarber, and Robert W. Oldendick. 1978. "Change in the Structure of American Political Attitudes: The Nagging Question of Question Wording." *American Journal of Political Science* 22 (2): 250–69.

Blais, André, and Robert Young. 1999. "Why Do People Vote? An Experiment in Rationality." *Public Choice* 99 (1–2): 39–55.

Bleemer, Zachary, Meta Brown, Donghoon Lee, and Wilbert van Der Klaauw. 2014. "Debt, Jobs, or Housing: What's Keeping Millennials at Home?" Federal Reserve Bank of New York Staff Report No. 700.

Bogard, Cynthia J., Ian Sheinheit, and Renee P. Clarke. 2008. "Information They Can Trust: Increasing Youth Voter Turnout at the University." *PS: Political Science and Politics* 41 (3): 541–46.

Boulding, William, Ajay Kalra, Richard Staelin, and Valarie A. Zeithaml. 1993. "A Dynamic Process Model of Service Quality: From Expectations to Behavioral Intentions." *Journal of Marketing Research* 30: 7–27.

Bowler, Shaun, and Todd Donovan. 1994. "Information and Opinion Change on Ballot Measures." *Political Behavior* 16 (4): 411–35.

———. 1998. *Demanding Choices: Opinion, Voting and Direct Democracy.* Ann Arbor: University of Michigan Press.

———. 2008. "Barriers to Participation for Whom? Regulations on Voting and Uncompetitive Elections." *Designing Democratic Government: Making Institutions Work* 4: 40.

Bowler, Shaun, Todd Donovan, and Trudi Happ. 1992. "Ballot Propositions and Information Costs: Direct Democracy and the Fatigued Voter." *The Western Political Quarterly* 45 (2): 559–68.

Bowler, Shaun, Stephen P. Nicholson, and Gary M. Segura. 2006. "Earthquakes and Aftershocks: Race, Direct Democracy, and Partisan Change." *American Journal of Political Science* 50 (1): 146–59.

Brady, Henry E., and John E. McNulty. 2011. "Turnout Out to Vote: The Costs of Finding and Getting to the Polling Place." *The American Political Science Review* 105 (1): 115–34.

Brady, Henry E., Guy-Uriel Charles, Benjamin Highton, Martha Kropf, Walter R. Mebane, Jr., and Michael Traugott. 2004. *Interim Report on Alleged Irregularities in the United States Presidential Election of 2 November 2004.* New York: Social Science Research Council. https://www.verifiedvoting.org/downloads/InterimReport122204.pdf. Accessed October 23, 2017.

Brady, Henry E., Sidney Verba, and Kay Lehman Schlozman. 1995. "Beyond SES: A Resource Model of Political Participation." *American Political Science Review* 89 (2): 271–94.

Branton, Regina P. 2003. "Examining Individual-level Voting Behavior on State Ballot Propositions." *Political Research Quarterly* 56 (3): 367–77.

———. 2004. "Voting in Initiative Elections: Does the Context of Racial and Ethnic Diversity Matter?" *State Politics and Policy Quarterly* 4 (3): 294–317.

Brians, Craig Leonard, and Bernard Grofman. 1999. "When Registration Barriers Fall, Who Votes? An Empirical Test of a Rational Choice Model." *Public Choice* 99 (1–2): 161–76.

Brockington, David. 2003. "A Low Information Theory of Ballot Position Effect." *Political Behavior* 25 (1): 1–27.

Burden, Barry C., and Amber Wichowsky. 2014. "Economic Discontent as a Mobilizer: Unemployment and Voter Turnout." *Journal of Politics* 76 (4): 887–98.

Burnett, Craig M., Elizabeth Garrett, and Mathew D. McCubbins. 2010. "The Dilemma of Direct Democracy." *Election Law Journal* 9 (4): 305–24.

Burnett, Craig M., and Vladimir Kogan. 2010. "The Case of the Stolen Initiative: Were Voters Framed?" Paper Presented at the Annual Conference of the American Political Science Association, Washington, DC, September.

———. 2015. "When does Ballot Language Influence Voter Choices? Evidence from a Survey Experiment." *Political Communication* 32 (1): 109–26.

Cahoon, Delwin, and Ed M. Edmonds. 1980. "The Watched Pot Still Won't Boil: Expectancy as a Variable in Estimating the Passage of Time." *Bulletin of the Psychonomic Society* 16: 115–16.

Campbell, Angus, Phillip E. Converse, Warren E. Miller, and Donald E. Stokes. 1960. *The American Voter*. Chicago: University of Chicago Press.

Carmines, Edward G., and James A. Stimson. 1980. "The Two Faces of Issue Voting." *American Political Science Review* 74 (1): 78–91.

Carmon, Ziv, J. George Shanthikumar, and Tali F. Carmon. 1995. "A Psychological Perspective on Service Segmentation Models: The Significance of Accounting for Consumers' Perception of Waiting and Service." *Management Science* 41 (11): 1806–15.

Carmon, Ziv, and Daniel Kahneman. 1995. "The Experienced Utility of Queuing: Real-Time Affect and Retrospective Evaluations of Simulated Queues." Working paper, Fuqua School of Business, Duke University.

Chaum, David. 2004. "Secret-Ballot Receipts: True Voter-Verifiable Elections." *CryptoBytes* 7 (2): 13–26.

Citrin, Jack, and Donald Phillip Green. 1990. "The Self-Interest Motive in American Public Opinion." *Research in Micropolitics* 3: 1–28.

Claassen, Ryan L., David B. Magleby, J. Quin Monson, and Kelly D. Patterson. 2008. "'At Your Service': Voter Evaluations of Poll Worker Performance." *American Politics Research* 36 (4): 612–34.

———. 2013. "Voter Confidence and the Election-Day Voting Experience." *Political Behavior* 35 (2): 215–35.

Cobb, Kim, and Michael Hedges. 2004. "Large Voter Turnout Jams Polls." *Houston Chronicle*, November 3.

Cohen, Adam. 2012. "No One Should Have to Wait 7 Hours to Vote." *The Atlantic*, November 5.

Committee of Seventy. 2012. "Did Your Provisional Ballot Count?" Organization Publication, December 5. https://www.seventy.org/publications/2012/12/05/did-your-provisional-ballot-count. Accessed October 23, 2017.*Congressional Record*. 2005. January 6.

Conrad, Frederick G, Benjamin B. Bederson, Brian Lewis, Emilia Herrnson, and Richard G. Niemi. 2009. "Electronic Voting Eliminates Hanging Chads but Introduces New Usability Challenges." *International Journal of Human-Computer Studies* 67 (1): 111–24.

Cooper, Martha. 2016. "People are Already Documenting Extremely Long Lines at US Polling Places in Swing States" *Quartz*, November 8. https://qz.com/830647/ election-2016-people-are-already-documenting-extremely-long-lines-at-us-polling-places-in-swing-states/. Accessed October 23, 2017.

Costa, Dora L., and Matthew E. Kahn. 2003. "Civic Engagement and Community Heterogeneity: An Economist's Perspective." *Perspectives on Politics* 1 (1): 103–11.

Dao, James, Ford Fessenden, and Tom Zeller. 2004. "Voting Problems in Ohio Spur Call for Overhaul." *New York Times*, December 24.

Darcy, Robert, and A. L. Schneider. 1989. "Confusing Ballots, Roll-Off, and the Black Vote." *Western Political Quarterly* 42 (3): 347–64.

Darcy, Robert E. 1980. "Consensus, Constraint and Political Polarization in Recent Presidential Elections." *Political Behavior* 2 (2): 147–61.

Dermody, Janine, Stuart Hanmer-Lloyd, and Richard Scullion. 2010. "Young People and Voting Behaviour: Alienated Youth and (or) an Interested and Critical Citizenry?" *European Journal of Marketing* 44 (3/4): 421–35.

Dettrey, Bryan J. 2013. "Relative Losses and Economic Voting: Sociotropic Considerations or 'Keeping up with the Joneses?'" *Politics and Policy* 41 (5): 788–806.

DeWitt, Jeff, Richard Engstrom, Stephen Nicholson, and Shyam Sriram. 2005. "The City too Busy to Hate? Precinct Quality and Turnout in Atlanta." Paper presented at the Western Political Science Association Annual Meeting, Oakland, CA, March.

Dillman, Don A. 2000. *Mail and Internet Surveys: The Tailored Design Method.* 2nd Edition. New York: Wiley.

———. 2002. "Presidential Address: Navigating the Rapids of Change: Some Observations on Survey Methodology in the Early Twenty-First Century." *The Public Opinion Quarterly* 66 (3): 473–94.

Dimonick, Michael A., and Samuel L. Popkin. 1995. "Who Knows: Political Knowledge in Comparative Perspective." Paper presented at the Annual Meeting of the Midwest Political Science Association, Chicago, IL, April.

Doherty, David, and E. Scott Adler. 2014. "The Persuasive Effects of Partisan Campaign Mailers." *Political Research Quarterly* 67 (3): 562–73.

Donovan, Todd, and Shaun Bowler. 1998. "Direct Democracy and Minority Rights: An Extension." *American Journal of Political Science* 42 (3): 1020–24.

Donovan, Todd, and Jeffrey Karp. 2006. "Popular Support for Direct Democracy" *Party Politics* 12 (5): 671–88.

Donovan, Todd, Shaun Bowler, and David S. McCuan. 2001. "Political Consultants and the Initiative Industrial Complex." In *Dangerous Democracy*, edited by Larry J. Sabato, Howard R. Ernst, and Bruce A. Larson, 101–34. Lanham, MD: Rowman & Littlefield.

Donovan, Todd, Caroline J. Tolbert, and Daniel A. Smith. 2009. "Political Engagement, Mobilization, and Direct Democracy." *Public Opinion Quarterly* 73 (1): 98–118.

Donovan, Todd, Caroline Tolbert, Daniel A. Smith, and Janine A. Parry. 2005. "Did Gay Marriage Elect George W. Bush?" Paper presented at the State Politics Conference, East Lansing, MI, May.

Downs, Anthony. 1957. *An Economic Theory of Democracy.* New York: Harper.

Elmendorf, Christopher S., and Douglas M. Spencer. 2013. "Are Ballot Titles Biased: Partisanship in California's Supervision of Direct Democracy." *University of California Irvine Law Review* 3: 511.

Elsbach, Kmberly D., and Andrew B. Hargadon. 2006. "Enhancing Creativity through 'Mindless' Work: A Framework of Workday Design." *Organization Science* 17 (4): 470–83.

Everett, Sarah P., Michael D. Byrne, and Kristen K. Greene. 2006. "Measuring the Usability of Paper Ballots: Efficiency, Effectiveness, and Satisfaction." In *Proceedings of the Human Factors and Ergonomics Society Annual Meeting* 50 (24): 2547–51. Los Angeles: SAGE Publications.

Everhart, Michelle. 2016. "Ohio Politics Now: Thousands Wait in Line to Cast Vote before Election Day." *The Columbus Dispatch*, November 7.

Farr, James N., James J. Jenkins, and Donald G. Paterson. 1951. "Simplification of Flesch Reading Ease Formula." *Journal of Applied Psychology* 35 (5): 333–37.

Feige, Gerald M. 2005. "Refining the Vote: Suggested Amendments to the Help America Vote Act's Provisional Balloting Standards." *Penn State Law Review* 110: 449.

Fitrakis, Bob. 2014. "Soulless Secretary of State Targets those Voting While Black." *Columbus Free Press,* March 6.

Fitzgerald, Mary. 2003. "Easier Voting Methods Boost Youth Turnout." The Center for Information and Research on Civic Learning and Engagement (CIRCLE), February. http://www.civicyouth.org/PopUps/WorkingPapers/WP01Fitzgerald.pdf. Accessed October 23, 2017.

———. 2005. "Greater Convenience but Not Greater Turnout the Impact of Alternative Voting Methods on Electoral Participation in the United States." *American Politics Research* 33 (6): 842–67.

Flanders, Chad. 2006."Please Don't Cite This Case! The Precedential Value of Bush v. Gore." *Yale Law Journal Pocket Part* 116: 141–44.

Foley, Edward B. 2005."The Promise and Problems of Provisional Voting." *George Washington Law Review* 73.

———. 2008. "Uncertain Insurance: The Ambiguities and Complexities of Provisional Voting." *Ohio State Public Law Working Paper* 190.

Foreman, Lauren, John Spink, and Raisa Habersham. 2016. "Election Day in Atlanta: As Polls Close, Some Voters Went to Wrong Precinct." *Atlanta Journal-Constitution*, November 8.

Fraisse, Paul. 1963. *The Psychology of Time.* Westport, CT: Greenwood Press.

Franklin, Mark N. 1999. "Electoral Engineering and Cross-National Turnout Differences: What Role for Compulsory Voting?" *British Journal of Political Science* 29 (1): 205–16.

Gallup, George. 1941. "Question Wording in Public Opinion Polls." *Sociometry* 4 (3): 259–68.

Gamble, Barbara. 1997. "Putting Civil Rights to a Popular Vote." *American Journal of Political Science* 91 (1): 245–69.

Ganster, Daniel C. 2005. "Executive Job Demands: Suggestions from a Stress and Decision-Making Perspective." *Academy of Management Review* 30 (3): 492–502.

Gatrell, Jay, and Gregory Bierly. 2002. "Weather and Voter Turnout: Kentucky Primary and General Elections, 1990–2000." *Southeastern Geographer* 42: 114–34.

Gentry, Bobbi. 2010. *Why Youth Vote: Identity, Inspirational Leaders, and Independence.* New York: City University of New York.

George, Alexander L. 1980. *Presidential Decision Making in Foreign Policy: The Effective Use of Information and Advice.* Boulder, CO: Westview Press.

Gerber, Alan S., Gregory A. Huber, David Doherty, Conor M. Dowling, and Seth J. Hill. 2013. "Who Wants to Discuss Vote Choices with Others?" *Public Opinion Quarterly* 77 (3): 474–96.

Gerber, Alan S., Dean Karlan, and Daniel Bergan. 2009. "Does the Media Matter? A Field Experiment Measuring the Effect of Newspapers on Voting Behavior and Political Opinions." *Applied Economics* 1 (2): 35–52.

Getmansky, Anna, and Thomas Zeitoff. 2014. "Terrorism and Voting: The Effect of Rocket Threat on Voting in Israeli Elections." *American Political Science Review* 108 (3): 588–604.

Gibson, John, Bonggeun Kim, Steven Stillman, and Geua Boe-Gibson. 2013. "Time to Vote?" *Public Choice* 156 (3/4): 517–36.

Gimpel, James G., and Jason E. Schuknecht. 2003. "Political Participation and the Accessibility of the Ballot Box." *Political Geography* 22: 471–88.

Goel, Madad Lal, and Lester Milbrath. 1977. *Political Participation.* 2nd Edition. Chicago: Rand McNally College Publishing Co.

Goldman, Jonah H. 2005. "Partisanship, Problems, and Promise-The Role of the 2004 Election in Shaping the Reform Debate." *Human Rights* 32 (4): 4–5.

Gomez, Brad T., Thomas G. Hansford, and George A. Krause. 2007. "The Republicans Should Pray for Rain: Weather, Turnout, and Voting in the U.S." *Journal of Politics* 69 (3): 649–63.

Green, Donald P., and Alan S. Gerber. 2008. *Get Out the Vote: How to Increase Voter Turnout.* 2nd Edition. Washington, DC: Brookings Institute Press.

Groves, Robert M., Stanley Presser, and Sarah Dipko. 2004. "The Role of Topic Interest in Survey Participation Decisions." *Public Opinion Quarterly,* 68 (1): 2–31.

Groves, Robert M., and Nancy H. Fultz. 1985. "Gender Effects among Telephone Interviewers in a Survey of Economic Attitudes." *Sociological Methods & Research* 14 (1): 31–52.

Gunn, Priscilla F. 1981. "Initiatives and Referendums: Direct Democracy and Minority Interests." *Urban Law Annual* 22: 135.

Haider-Markel, Donald P., Alana Querze, and Kara Lindaman. 2007. "Lose, Win, or Draw? A Reexamination of Direct Democracy and Minority Rights." *Political Research Quarterly* 60 (2): 304–14.

Hajnal, Zoltan L., Elisabeth R. Gerber, and Hugh Louch. 2002. "Minorities and Direct Legislation: Evidence from California Ballot Proposition Elections." *The Journal of Politics* 64 (1): 154–77.

Hall, Thad E., J. Quin Monson, and Kelly D. Patterson. 2009. "The Human Dimension of Elections How Poll Workers Shape Public Confidence in Elections." *Political Research Quarterly* 62 (3): 507–22.

Hambrick, Donald C., Sydney Finkelstein, and Ann C. Mooney. 2005. "Executive Job Demands: New Insights for Explaining Strategic Decisions and Leader Behaviors." *Academy of Management Review* 30 (3): 472–91.

Hannigan, John A. 1985. "The Armalite and the Ballot Box: Dilemmas of Strategy and Ideology in the Provisional IRA." *Social Problems* 33 (1): 31–40.

Hare, Christopher, and Keith T Poole. 2014. "The Polarization of Contemporary American Politics." *Polity* 46 (3): 411–29.

Harmon, Steven. 2010. "Key Ruling Throws Out Claim that Prop. 25 Would Protect Two-Thirds Vote on Taxes." *Mercury News*, August 5.

Haspel, Moshe, and H. Gibbs Knotts. 2005. "Location, Location, Location: Precinct Placement and the Costs of Voting." *The Journal of Politics* 67 (2): 560–73.

Hastings, Jeff, and Damon Cann. 2014. "Ballot Titles and Voter Decision Making on Ballot Questions." *State and Local Government Review* 46 (2): 118–27.

Hero, Rodney. 1998. *Faces of Inequality: Social Diversity in American Politics*. New York: Oxford University Press.

Hero, Rodney E., and Caroline J. Tolbert. 2004. "Minority Voices and Citizen Attitudes about Government Responsiveness in the American States: Do Social and Institutional Context Matter?" *British Journal of Political Science* 34 (1): 109–21.

Hermann, Margaret G. 1979. "Indicators of Stress in Policymakers during Foreign Policy Crises." *Political Psychology* 1 (1): 27–46.

Herrnson, Paul S., Michael J. Hanmer, and Richard G. Niemi. 2012. "The Impact of Ballot Type on Voter Errors." *American Journal of Political Science* 56 (3): 716–30.

Herrnson, Paul S., Ryan L. Claassen, Richard G. Niemi, and Kelly D. Patterson. 2013. "Exceeding Expectations? Determinants of Satisfaction with the Voting Process in the 2008 U.S. Presidential Election." *The Journal of Politics* 75 (2): 451–63.

Hershatter, Andrea, and Molly Epstein. 2010. "Millennials and the World of Work: An Organization and Management Perspective." *Journal of Business and Psychology* 25 (2): 211–23.

Herzog, A. Regula, and Jerald G. Bachman. 1981. "Effects of Questionnaire Length on Response Quality." *Public Opinion Quarterly* 45 (4): 549–59.

Highton, Benjamin. 2006. "Long Lines, Voting Machine Availability, and Turnout: The Case of Franklin County, Ohio in the 2004 Presidential Election." *PS: Political Science and Politics* 39 (1): 65–68.

Hill, Kim Quaile, and Jan E. Leighley. 1993. "Party Ideology, Organization, and Competitiveness as Mobilizing Forces in Gubernatorial Elections." *American Journal of Political Science* 37 (4): 1158–78.

———. 1994. "Mobilizing Institutions and Class Representation in U.S. State Electorates." *Political Research Quarterly* 47 (1): 137–50.

Hill, Kim Quaile, and Jan E. Leighley. 1996. "Political Parties and Class Mobilization in Contemporary United States Elections." *American Journal of Political Science* 40 (3): 787–804.

Hobolt, Sara, James Tilley, and Jill Wittrock. 2013. "Listening to the Government: How Information Shapes Responsibility Attributions." *Political Behavior* 35 (1): 153–74.

Hockey, G. Robert J. 1970. "Effects of Loud Noise on Attentional Selectivity." *Quarterly Journal of Experimental Psychology* 22 (1): 28–36.

Holsti, Ole R. 1984. "Theories of Crisis Decision Making." In *International Conflict and Conflict Management: Readings in World Politics*, edited by Robert O. Matthews, Arthur G. Rubinoff, and Janice Gross Stein, 65–83. Ontario: Prentice-Hall.

Hood, M. V., and Charles S. Bullock. 2008. "Worth a Thousand Words? An Analysis of Georgia's Voter Identification Statute." *American Politics Research* 36 (4): 555–79.

———. 2012. "Much Ado about Nothing? An Empirical Assessment of the Georgia Voter Identification Statute." *State Politics and Policy Quarterly* 12 (4): 394–414.

Hopkins, Daniel J. 2011. "Translating into Votes: The Electoral Impacts of Spanish-Language Ballots." *American Journal of Political Science* 55 (4): 814–30.

Huckfeldt, Robert, and John Sprague. 1992. "Political Parties and Electoral Mobilization: Political Structure, Social Structure, and the Party Canvass." *The American Political Science Review* 86 (1): 70–86.

Hui, Michael K., Mrugank V. Thakor, and Ravi Gill. 1998. "The Effect of Delay Type and Service Stage on Consumers' Reactions to Waiting." *Journal of Consumer Research* 24 (4): 469–79.

Im, Tobin. 2009. "An Exploratory Study of Time Stress and Its Causes among Government Employees." *Public Administration Review* 69 (1): 104–115.

Indridason, Indridi H. 2014. "The Collapse: Economic Considerations in Vote Choice in Iceland." *Journal of Elections, Public Opinion and Parties* 24 (2): 134–59.

Janakiraman, Narayan, Robert J. Meyer, and Stephen J. Hoch. 2011. "The Psychology of Decisions to Abandon Waits for Service." *Journal of Marketing Research* 48 (6): 970–84.

Janis, Irving. 1982. "Decision-Making Under Stress." In *Handbook of Stress: Theoretical and Clinical Aspects*, edited by L. Goldberger and S. Breznitz, 69–80. New York: Free Press.

Janis, Irving, and Leon Mann. 1977. *Decision Making: A Psychological Analysis of Conflict, Choice, and Commitment.* New York: Free Press.

Janis, Irving, Peter Defares, and Paul Grossman. 1982. "Hypervigilant Reactions to Threat." In *Selye's Guide to Stress Research, Volume 3*, edited by H. Selye. New York: Van Nostrand Reinhold.

Kahn, Kim Fridkin, and Patrick J. Kenney. 2004. *No Holds Barred: Negativity in U.S. Senate Campaigns.* Upper Saddle River, NJ: Pearson Education.

Kahneman, Daniel. 1973. *Attention and Effort.* Englewood Cliffs, NJ: Prentice-Hall.

Kaiser, Hans, and Bob Moore. 2001. "Voting Behavior and the 2002 Elections." *Campaigns and Elections* 22 (9): 23.

Kalton, Graham, Martin Collins, and Lindsay Brook. 1978. "Experiments in Wording Opinion Questions." *Applied Statistics* 27 (2): 149–61.

Kane, Emily W., and Laura J. Macaulay. 1993. "Interviewer Gender and Gender Attitudes." *Public Opinion Quarterly* 57 (1): 1–28.

Keinan, Giora. 1987. "Decision Making Under Stress: Scanning of Alternatives under Controllable and Uncontrollable Threats." *Journal of Personality and Social Psychology* 52 (3): 639–44.

Kelley, Stanley, Richard E. Ayres, and William G. Bowen. 1967. "Registration and Voting: Putting First Things First." *American Political Science Review* 61 (2): 359–79.

Key, Vladimir O. Jr. 1949. *Southern Politics in State and Nation.* New York: Alfred Knopf.

———. 1964. *Public Opinion and American Democracy.* New York: Wiley.

Kidd, Quentin, Herman Diggs, Mehreen Farooq, and Megan Murray. 2007. "Black Voters, Black Candidates, and Social Issues: Does Party Identification Matter?" *Social Science Quarterly* 88 (1): 165–76.

Kim, Jae-On, John R. Petrocik, and Stephen N. Enokson. 1975. "Voter Turnout among the American States: Systemic and Individual Components." *American Political Science Review* 69 (1): 107–24.

Kimball, David C., and Edward B. Foley. 2009. "Unsuccessful Provisional Voting in the 2008 General Election." *Pew Center on the States, Provisional Ballots: An Imperfect Solution.*

Kimball, David C., and Martha Kropf. 2005. "Ballot Design and Unrecorded Votes on Paper-Based Ballots." *Public Opinion Quarterly* 69 (4): 508–29.

———. 2006. "Ballot Initiatives and Residual Ballots in the 2004 Presidential Election." Paper presented at the Annual Meeting of the Southern Political Science Association, Atlanta, GA, January.

Kimball, David C., Martha Kropf, and Lindsay Battles. 2006. "Helping America Vote? Election Administration, Partisanship, and Provisional Voting in the 2004 Election." *Election Law Journal* 5 (4): 447–61.

Kincaid, J. Peter, Robert P. Fishburne Jr., Richard L. Rogers, and Brad S. Chissom. 1975. *Derivation of New Readability Formulas: Automated Readability Index, Fog Count, and Flesch Reading Ease Formula.* Memphis, TN: Naval Air Station.

Knack, Stephen. 1995. "Does 'Motor Voter' Work? Evidence from State Level Data." *Journal of Politics* 57 (3): 796–811.

Knack, Stephen, and Martha Kropf. 2003. "Roll Off at the Top of the Ballot: International Undervoting in American Presidential Elections." *Politics & Policy* 31 (4): 575–94.

Knapp, Joe. 2004. "Effect of Voting-Machine Allocations on the 2004 Election – Franklin County, Ohio." www.prism.gatech.edu/~bt71/mgt3501/queue%20to%20 vote.pdf.

Kowalski-Trakofler, Kathleen M., Charles Vaught, and Ted Scharf. 2003. "Judgment and Decision Making under Stress: An Overview for Emergency Managers." *International Journal of Emergency Management* 1 (3): 278–89.

Kramer, Gerald. 1971. "The Effects of Precinct-level Canvassing on Voter Behavior." *Public Opinion Quarterly* 34 (4): 560–72.

Krassa, Michael A. 1988. "Context and the Canvass: The Mechanisms of Interactions." *Political Behavior* 10 (Autumn): 233–46.

———. 1989. "Getting Out the Black Vote: The Party Canvass and the Black Response." In *New Perspectives in American Politics*, edited by Lucius Barker (special issue). *National Political Science Review* 1: 58–75.

Kropf, Martha, and David C. Kimball. 2013. *Helping America Vote: The Limits of Election Reform*. New York: Routledge.

Laskowski, Sharon J., and Janice (Ginny) Redish. 2006. "Making Ballot Language Understandable to Voters." *Electronic Voting Technology*: 1–6.

Lau, Richard. R., and David P. Redlawsk. 1997. "Voting Correctly." *American Political Science Review* 91 (3): 585–99.

———. 2006. *How Voters Decide: Information Processing in Elections Campaigns*. Cambridge: Cambridge University Press.

Laurent, André. 1972. "Effects of Question Length on Reporting Behavior in the Survey Interview." *Journal of the American Statistical Association* 67 (338): 298–305.

Lausen, Marcia. 2008. *Design for Democracy: Ballot and Election Design*. Chicago: University of Chicago Press.

Leclerc, France, Berndt H. Schmitt, and Laurette Dube. 1995. "Waiting Time and Decision Making: Is Time Like Money?" *Journal of Consumer Research* 22 (1): 110–19.

Leighley, Jan E., and Jonathan Nagler. 1992. "Individual and Systemic Influences on Turnout: Who Votes? 1984." *Journal of Politics* 54 (3): 718–40.

———. 1992. "Socioeconomic Class Bias in Turnout, 1964–1988: The Voters Remain the Same." *American Political Science Review* 86 (3): 725–36.

———. 2007. "Unions, Voter Turnout, and Class Bias in the U.S. Electorate, 1964–2004." *Journal of Politics* 69 (20): 430–41.

Lewin, Kurt. 1943. "Defining the Field at a Given Time." *Psychological Review* 50 (May): 292–310.

Lewis, Daniel C. 2011. "Direct Democracy and Minority Rights: Same Sex Marriage Bans in the US States." *Social Science Quarterly* 92 (2): 364–83.

Liebschutz, Sarah F., and Daniel J. Palazzolo. 2005. "HAVA and the States." *Publius: The Journal of Federalism* 35 (4): 497–514.

Lin II, Rong-Gong. 2016. "Will My Provisional Vote Really be Counted?" *Los Angeles Times*, November 8.

Lipow, Arthur. 1973. "Plebiscitarian Politics and Progressivism: The Direct Democracy Movement." Paper presented at the Annual Meeting of the American Historical Association, San Francisco, CA, December.

Liptak, Adam. 2004. "Voting Problems in Ohio Set off an Alarm." *The New York Times,* November 7.

Lott, John R. 2006. "Evidence of Voter Fraud and the Impact that Regulations to Reduce Fraud have on Voter Participation Rates." (Available at SSRN 925611).

Lueptow, Lloyd B., Susan L. Moser, and Brian F. Pendleton. 1990. "Gender and Response Effects in Telephone Interviews about Gender Characteristics." *Sex Roles* 22 (1): 29–42.

Lupia, Arthur. 1994a. "Shortcuts Versus Encyclopedias: Information and Voting Behavior in California Insurance Reform Elections." *American Political Science Review* 88 (1): 63–76.

———. 1994b. "The Effect of Information on Voting Behavior and Electoral Outcomes: An Experimental Study of Direct Legislation." *Public Choice* 78 (1): 65–86.

———. 2001. "Dumber than Chimps? An Assessment of Direct Democracy Voters, in *Dangerous Democracy*." In *The Battle over Ballot Initiatives in America*, edited by Larry J. Sabato, H. R. Ernst, and B. A. Larson, 66–70. Lanham, MD: Rowman & Littlefield.

Magleby, David B. 1984. *Direct Legislation: Voting on Ballot Propositions in the United States*. Baltimore: Johns Hopkins University Press.

Maister, David. 1985. "The Psychology of Waiting Lines." In *The Service Encounter*, edited by John Czepiel, Michael R. Solomon, and Carol Suprenant. Lexington, MA: D. C. Heath and Company.

Mandelbaum, Avishai, and Nahum Shimkin. 2000. "A Model for Rational Abandonment from Invisible Queues." *Queuing Systems: Theory and Applications* 36 (1): 141–73.

McClurg, Scott. 2006. "Political Disagreement in Context: The Conditional Effect of Neighborhood Context, Disagreement and Political Talk on Electoral Participation." *Political Behavior* 28 (4): 349–66.

McDonald, Michael P. 2004. "Up, Up and Away! Voter Participation in the 2004 Presidential Election." *The Forum* 2 (4).

McDonald, Michael P., and John Samples. 2006. "The Marketplace of Democracy: Normative and Empirical Issues." In *The Marketplace of Democracy: Electoral Competition and American Politics*, edited by Michael P. McDonald and John Samples, 1–24. Washington, DC: Brookings Institute Press.

McNulty, John E., Conor M. Dowling, and Margaret H. Ariotti. 2009. "Driving Saints to Sin: How Increasing the Difficulty of Voting Dissuades Even the Most Motivated Voters." *Political Analysis* 17 (4): 435–55.

Meredith, Marc, and Neil Maihotia. 2011. "Convenience Voting Can Affect Election Outcomes." *Election Law Journal* 10 (3): 227–53.

Merriam, Charles E., and Harold F. Gosnell. 1924. *Non-Voting: Causes and Methods of Control*. Chicago: University of Chicago Press.

Meyer, Thierry. 1994. "Subjective Importance of Goal and Reactions to Waiting in Line." *Journal of Social Psychology* 134 (December): 819–27.

Milita, Kerri. 2015. "Election Laws and Agenda Setting: How Election Law Restrictiveness Shapes the Complexity of State Ballot Measures." *State Politics and Policy Quarterly* 15 (2): 119–46.

Miller, Elizabeth Gelfand, Barbara E. Kahn, and Mary Frances Luce. 2008. "Consumer Wait Management Strategies for Negative Service Events: A Coping Approach." *Journal of Consumer Research* 34 (5): 635–48.

Miller, Mark Crispin. 2005. "None Dare Call it Stolen." *Harper's Magazine*.

Mondak, Jeffrey J. 1995. "Newspapers and Political Awareness." *American Journal of Political Science* 39 (2): 513–27.

Montjoy, Robert S. 2008. "The Public Administration of Elections." *Public Administration Review* 68 (5): 788–99.

Mutz, Diana C. 2002. "The Consequences of Cross-Cutting Networks for Political Participation." *American Journal of Political Science* 46 (4): 838–55.

———. 2006. *Hearing the Other Side: Deliberative versus Participatory Democracy*. Cambridge: Cambridge University Press.

Myers, John. 2017. "There were Serious Problems in 2016 for Some California Voters Who Don't Speak English, New Report Says." *Los Angeles Times*, May 10.

Myers, Karen K., and Kamyab Sadaghiani. 2010. "Millennials in the Workplace: A Communication Perspective on Millennials' Organizational Relationships and Performance." *Journal of Business and Psychology* 25 (2): 225–38.

Neiheisel, Jacob R., and Barry C. Burden. 2012. "The Impact of Election Day Registration on Voter Turnout and Election Outcomes." *American Politics Research* 40 (4): 636–64.

Ng, Eddy S. W., Linda Schweitzer, and Sean T. Lyons. 2010. "New Generation, Great Expectations: A Field Study of the Millennial Generation." *Journal of Business and Psychology* 25 (2): 281–92.

Nichols, Stephen M., and Gregory A. Strizek. 1995. "Electronic Voting Machines and Ballot Roll-Off." *American Politics Quarterly,* 23 (3): 300–18.

Nicholson, Stephen P. 2003. "The Political Environment and Ballot Proposition Awareness." *American Journal of Political Science* 47 (3): 403–10.

———. 2005. *Voting the Agenda: Candidates, Elections and Ballot Measures*. Princeton, NJ: Princeton University Press.

Nie, Winter. 2000. "Waiting: Integrating Social and Psychological Perspectives in Operations Management." *Omega: The International Journal of Management Science* 28 (6): 611–29.

Niemen, Jayme, Karl Giuseffi, Kevin Smith, Jeffrey French, Israel Waismel-Manor, and John Hibbing. 2015. "Voting at Home is Associated with Lower Cortisol than Voting at the Polls." *PLoS One* 10 (9). doi:10.1371/ journal.pone.0135289.

Niemi, Richard G., and Paul S. Herrnson. 2003. "Beyond the Butterfly: The Complexity of US Ballots." *Perspectives on Politics* 1 (2): 317–26.

Osuna, Edgar Elias. 1985. "The Psychological Cost of Waiting." *Journal of Mathematical Psychology* 29: 82–105.

Pacheco, Julianna Sandell. 2008. "Political Socialization in Context: The Effect of Political Competition on Youth Voter Turnout." *Political Behavior* 30 (4): 415–36.

Palast, Greg, and Dennis J. Bernstein. 2016. "Placebo Ballots: Stealing California From Bernie Using an Old GOP Vote-Snatching Trick." *Reader Supported News*, June 1. http://readersupportednews.org/opinion2/277-75/37203-placebo-ballots-stealing-california-from-bernie-using-an-old-gop-vote-snatching-trick. Accessed October 23, 2017.

Palm, Conny. 1953. "Methods of Judging the Annoyance Caused by Congestion." *TELE* 2: 1–20.

Parent, Wayne, and Wesley Shrum. 1985. "Critical Electoral Success and Black Voter Registration: An Elaboration of the Voter Consent Model." *Social Science Quarterly* 66 (3): 695–703.

Pattie, Charles J., and Ronald J. Johnston. 2009. "Conversation, Disagreement and Political Participation." *Political Behavior* 31 (2): 261–85.

Payne, John W., James R. Bettman, and Eric J. Johnson. 1988. "Adaptive Strategy Selection in Decision Making." *Journal of Experimental Psychology: Learning, Memory, and Cognition* 14 (3): 534.

Pearce, Matt. 2016. "'It Was Just Chaos': Broken Machines, Incomplete Voter Rolls Leave Some Wondering Whether Their Ballots Will Count." *Los Angeles Times,* June 7.

Persily, Nathaniel. 2005. "Options and Strategies for Renewal of Section 5 of the Voting Rights Act." *Howard Law Journal* 49: 717.

The Pew Center on the States. 2009. "Provisional Ballots: An Imperfect Solution." Issue Brief, *Pew Center.* July 23. http://www.pewtrusts.org/~/media/legacy/uploadedfiles/pcs_assets/2009/elecprovballotbrief0709pdf.pdf. Accessed October 23, 2017.

Pillsbury. A. J. 1931. "The Initiative, Its Achievements and Abuses." *Commonwealth – Part II* 25: 426–33.

Pitts, Michael J. 2008. "Empirically Assessing the Impact of Photo Identification at the Polls through an Examination of Provisional Balloting." *Journal of Law and Politics* 24: 475–527.

———. 2013. "Photo ID, Provisional Balloting, and Indiana's 2012 Primary Election." *University of Richmond Law Review* 47 (3): 939–60.

Piven, Frances Fox, and Richard A. Cloward. 1988. "National Voter Registration Reform: How it Might be Won." *PS: Political Science and Politics* 21 (4): 868–75.

Piyush, Kumar, Manahar U. Kalwani, and Maqbool Dada. 1997. "The Impact of Waiting Time Guarantees on Customers' Waiting Experiences." *Marketing Science* 16 (4): 295–314.

Pleschberger, Werner. 2017. "Making Informed Citizens in Local Direct Democracy. What Part Does Their Government Perform?" In *Local Government and Urban Governance in Europe*, 233–59. New York: Springer International Publishing.

Pompilio, Natalie. 2016. "Long Lines, Registration Issues Complicate Voting at Temple University." *The Washington Post,* November 8.

Powell, G. Bingham, Jr. 1986. "American Voter Turnout in Comparative Perspective." *The American Political Science Review* 80 (1): 17–43.

Powell, Michael, and Peter Slevin. 2004. "Several Factors Contributed to 'Lost' Voters in Ohio." *Washington Post,* December 15.

Ramirez, Steven A., and Aliza Organick. 2007. "Taking Voting Rights Seriously: Race and the Integrity of Democracy in America." *North Illinois University Law Review* 27 (3): 427.

Ranney, Austin. 1968. "The Representativeness of Primary Electorates." *Midwest Journal of Political Science* 12 (2): 224–38.

Rasinski, Kenneth A. 1989. "The Effect of Question Wording on Public Support for Government Spending." *Public Opinion Quarterly* 53 (3): 388–94.

Reilly, Shauna. 2010. *Design Meaning and Choice in Direct Democracy: Petitioners and Voters' Influence*. Farnham, UK: Ashgate.

———. 2015. *Language Assistance under the Voting Rights Act*. Lanham, MD: Lexington Books.

Reilly, Shauna, and Sean Richey. 2011. "Language Complexity and Roll-off: Does Ballot Question Readability Impact Participation?" *Political Research Quarterly* 64 (1): 59–67.

Reilly, Shauna, Sean Richey, and J. Benjamin Taylor. 2012. "Using Google Search Data for State Politics Research: An Empirical Validity Test Using Roll-off Data." *State Politics and Policy Quarterly* 12 (2): 146–59.

Reynolds, Andrew, and Marco Steenbergen. 2006. "How the World Votes: The Political Consequences of Ballot Design, Innovation and Manipulation." *Electoral Studies* 25 (3): 570–98.

Richey, Sean. 2008. "The Social Basis of Voting Correctly." *Political Communication* 25 (4): 366–76.

———. 2013. "Random and Systematic Error in Voting in Presidential Elections." *Political Research Quarterly* 66 (3): 645–57.

Riker, William H., and Peter C. Ordeshook. 1968. "A Theory of the Calculus of Voting." *American Political Science Review* 62 (1): 25–42.

Ritti, Richard. 1971. "Job Enrichment and Skill Utilization in Engineering Organization." In *New Perspective in Job Enrichment*, edited by John R. Maher, 131–56. New York: Van Nostrand.

Robinson, John P., and Geoffrey Godbey. 1998. "Trend, Gender, and Status Differences in Americans' Perceived Stress." *Society and Leisure* 21: 473–88.

Rosenstone, Steven, and John M. Hansen. 1993. *Mobilization, Participation and Democracy in America*. New York: Macmillan.

Rutchick, Abraham. 2010. "Deus Ex Machina: The Influence of Polling Place on Voting Behavior." *Political Psychology* 31 (2): 209–25.

Ryan, John Barry. 2011. "Social Networks as a Shortcut to Correct Voting." *American Journal of Political Science* 55 (4): 753–66.

Salisbury, Robert H., and Gordon Black. 1963. "Class and Party in Partisan and Non-Partisan Elections: The Case of Des Moines." *American Political Science Review* 57 (3): 584–92.

Santos, Fernanda. 2016. "Angry Arizona Voters Demand: Why Such Long Lines at Polling Sites?" *The New York Times*, March 25.

Sasser, W. Earl, R. Paul Olsen, and D. Daryl Wyckoff. 1978. *Management of Service Operations: Text, Cases, and Readings*. Boston: Allyn and Bacon.

Schmidt, David D. 1989. *Citizen Lawmakers: The Ballot Initiative Revolution*. Philadelphia: Temple University Press.

Shachar, Ron, and Barry Nalebuff. 1999. "Follow the Leader: Theory and Evidence on Political Participation." *The American Economic Review* 89 (June): 525–47.

Shambon, Leonard, and Keith Abouchar. 2006. "Trapped by Precincts: The Help America Vote Act's Provisional Ballots and the Problem of Precincts." *New York University Journal of Legislature and Public Policy* 10: 133–193.

Shapiro, Andrew L. 1993. "Challenging Criminal Disenfranchisement under the Voting Rights Act: A New Strategy." *The Yale Law Journal* 103 (2): 537–66.

Shimkin, Nahum, and Avishai Manelbaum. 2002. "Rational Abandonment from Tele-Queues: Nonlinear Waiting Costs with Heterogenous Preferences." *Queuing Systems* 47 (1): 1–30.

Sieber, John E. 1974. "Effects of Decision Importance on Ability to Generate Warranted Subjective Uncertainty." *Journal of Personality and Social Psychology* 5 (3): 688–94.

Sigelman, Lee, and Dixie Mercer McNeil. 1980. "White House Decision-Making under Stress: A Case Analysis." *American Journal of Political Science* 24 (4): 652–73.

Sinclair, Betsy, Thad E. Hall, and R. Michael Alvarez. 2011. "Flooding the Vote: Hurricane Katrina and Voter Participation in New Orleans." *American Politics Research* 39 (5): 921–57.

Singer, Matthew. 2011. "When Do Voters Actually Think "It's the Economy"? Evidence from the 2008 Presidential Campaign." *Electoral Studies* 30 (4): 621–32.

Sokhey, Edward, and Scott D. McClurg. 2012. "Social Networks and Correct Voting." *Journal of Politics* 74 (3): 751–64.

Stein, Robert M., and Greg Vonnahme. 2008. "Engaging the Unengaged Voter: Vote Centers and Voter Turnout." *Journal of Politics* 70 (2): 487–97.

Stevens, Daniel, John Sullivan, Barbara Allen, and Dean Alger. 2008. "What's Good for the Goose is Bad for the Gander: Negative Political Advertising, Partisanship, and Turnout." *Journal of Politics* 70 (2): 527–41.

Stewart III, Charles. 2009. *Early- and Late-Adopters of Provisional Ballots.* Washington, DC: Pew Center on the States, 1–4.

Stockfisch, Jerome R. 2012. "Amendments Might Need Warning Label." *The Tampa Tribune,* September 28.

Subar, Amy F., Regina G. Ziegler, Frances E. Thompson, Christine Cole Johnson, Joel L. Weissfeld, Douglas Reding, Katherine H. Kavounis, and Richard B. Hayes. 2001. "Is Shorter Always Better? Relative Importance of Questionnaire Length and Cognitive Ease on Response Rates and Data Quality for Two Dietary Questionnaires." *American Journal of Epidemiology* 153 (4): 404–409.

Sweeney, Richard T. 2005. "Reinventing Library Buildings and Services for the Millennial Generation." *Library Administration and Management* 19 (4): 165–76.

Sweeney, Richard. 2006. "Millennial Behaviors and Demographics." *Newark: New Jersey Institute of Technology* 12 (3): 10.

Taebel, Delbert A. 1975. "The Effect of Ballot Position on Electoral Success." *American Journal of Political Science* 19 (3): 519–26.

Taylor, Shirley. 1994. "Waiting for Service: The Relationships Between Delays and Evaluations of Service." *Journal of Marketing* 58 (April): 56–69.

Testa, Paul F., Matthew V. Hibbing, and Melinda Ritchie. 2014. "Orientations Toward Conflict and the Conditional Effects of Political Disagreement." *The Journal of Politics* 76 (3): 770–85.

Toch, Hans, and Kathleen Maguire. 2014. "Public Opinion Regarding Crime, Criminal Justice, and Related Topics: A Retrospect." *Journal of Research in Crime and Delinquency* 51 (4): 424–44.

Tokaji, Daniel P. 2008. "An Unsafe Harbor: Recounts, Contests, and the Electoral College." *Michigan Law Review First Impressions* 106: 84–117.

Tolbert, Caroline J., and Daniel A. Smith. 2004. "The Educative Effects of Ballot Initiatives on Voter Turnout." *American Political Research* 33 (2): 283–309.

Tolbert, Caroline J., and Rodney E. Hero. 1996. "Race/Ethnicity and Direct Democracy: An Analysis of California's Illegal Immigration Initiative." *The Journal of Politics* 58 (3): 806–18.

Trawalter, Sophie, Vicki S. Chung, Amy S. DeSantis, Clarissa D. Simon, and Emma K. Adam. 2012. "Physiological Stress Responses to the 2008 U.S. Presidential Election: The Role of Policy Preferences and Social Dominance Orientation." *Group Processes and Intergroup Relations* 15 (4): 333–45.

Vanderleeuw, James M., and Richard L. Engstrom. 1987. "Race, Referendums, and Roll-off." *The Journal of Politics* 49 (4): 1081–92.

Vanderleeuw, James M., and Thomas E. Sowers. 2007. "Race, Roll-Off, and Racial Transition: The Influence of Political Change on Racial Group Voter Roll-Off in Urban Elections." *Social Science Quarterly* 88 (4): 937–52.

Vecchione, Michele, Gianvittorio Caprara, Francesco Dentale, and Shalom H. Schwartz. 2013. "Voting and Values: Reciprocal Effects over Time." *Political Psychology* 34 (4): 465–85.

Verba, Sidney, and Norman H. Nie. 1972. *Participation in America: Political Democracy and Social Equality.* New York: Harper and Row.

Verba, Sidney, Kay Lehman Schlozman, and Henry E. Brady. 1995. *Voice and Equality: Civic Voluntarism in American Politics.* Boston: Harvard University Press.

Wachtel, Paul L. 1967. "Conceptions of Broad and Narrow Attention." *Psychological Bulletin* 68 (6): 417–29.

Waismel-Manor, Israel S., Gal Ifergane, and Hagit Cohen. 2011. "When Endocrinology and Democracy Collide: Emotions, Cortisol and Voting at National Elections." *European Neuropsychopharmacology* 21 (11): 789–95.

Walker, Jack L. 1996. "Ballot Forms and Voter Fatigue: An Analysis of the Office Block and Party Column Ballots." *Midwest Journal of Political Science* 10 (4): 448–63.

Wattenberg, Martin P., Ian McAllister, and Anthony Salvanto. 2000. "How Voting is Like Taking An Sat Test An Analysis of American Voter Roll-off." *American Politics Quarterly* 28 (2): 234–50.

Weiser, Wendy R. 2006. "Are HAVA's Provisional Ballots Working?" *U.S. Election Assistance Commission.* March 29. https://www.eac.gov/documents/2017/02/27/weiser-are-havas-provisional-ballots-working/. Accessed October 23, 2017.

Welch, Susan, and John Hibbing. 1992. "Financial Conditions, Gender, and Voting in American National Elections." *Journal of Politics* 54 (1): 197–213.

Weltman, Gershon, Janice E. Smith, and Glen H. Egstrom. 1971. "Perceptual Narrowing During Simulated Press-Chamber Exposure." *Human Factors* 13 (2): 99–107.

Weschle, Simon. 2014. "Two Types of Economic Voting: How Economic Conditions Jointly Affect Vote Choice and Turnout." *Electoral Studies* 34 (June): 39–53.

Wickens, Christopher D. 1996. "Designing for Stress." *Stress and Human Performance* 5 (1): 279–95.

Williams, Fay H. 1972. "Voting Barriers: Strategies for Removing Obstacles to the Black Ballot." *Black Law Journal* 2: 164.

Wright, Peter. 1974. "The Harassed Decision Maker: Time Pressures, Distractions, and the Use of Evidence." *Journal of Applied Psychology* 59 (5): 555–61.

Wright, Peter, and Barton Weitz. 1977. "Time Horizon Effects on Product Evaluation Strategies." *Journal of Marketing Research* 14 (4): 429–43.

Wolfinger, Raymond E., and Steven J. Rosenstone. 1978. "Effects of Registration Laws on Voter Turnout." *American Political Science Review* 72 (April): 245–56.

———. 1980. *Who Votes?* New Haven, CT: Yale University Press.

Zaller, John R. 1992. *The Nature and Origins of Mass Opinion.* Cambridge, MA: Cambridge University Press.

Index

Note: Page references for figures and tables are italicized

About the Authors

Shauna Reilly, PhD, Northern Kentucky University, focuses her research on political behavior and direct democracy in the American context. The majority of her research looks at accessibility of election materials to voters, with a particular interest in politics in the subnational context and the impact of race and ethnicity.

Stacy G. Ulbig, PhD, Sam Houston State University, focuses her research on questions about political attitudes and behavior, and the related topics of survey questionnaire design and public opinion in the American setting more generally.

Lightning Source UK Ltd.
Milton Keynes UK
UKHW02n1522130218
317826UK00003B/194/P

9 781498 533522